BECOMING AN INTRODUCTION MACHINE

Joseph RR Templin

Published by HG Creative Works, LLC.
Created and owned by JRRTOne Ring, LLC.
2024 edition.
All rights reserved.

BECOMING AN INTRODUCTION MACHINE

"How to Build an Introduction-Based Business in Under 90 Days"

Joseph RR Templin

Contents

About the author 1
Acknowledgements: 3
Background in Financial Services et al. 5
Some Numbers 11
    An Introduction is Valuable 15
    Americans Need You! 17
Process 19
    The Sales Cycle: 21
    The Process of Asking for Introductions 30
Will Set 35
    Activation Energy 38
    Discipline 40
    Training the Will 43
    This is Going to Suck 47
    Burn 48
    No Pill 49
    Passion as Fuel 51
    In Chaos Hides Opportunity 54
    1 Percent 56
    Trust The Process 57

One Bite	60
Welcome Class	64
Batman	67
Scantiest	69
Thankful	73
The Struggle is Real	75
Hannibal and The Way	77
Path of Most Resistance	79
Pain	81
Love It	83
Not Giving a F*ck	85
Not My Circus	89
Marathon	92
3 Rules	94
Championship Blues	97
Will And Work	99
Vent	101
Do Not Go Quietly	103
Will Power	105
Do Not Go Gently	108
90 Percent	110
Right Thing	114
Resiliency Defined	115
Resiliency	119
Limited Beliefs	122
Swim Like the Sharks	125
The Successful Psychopath	126
PARK	130

CONTENTS

Space Race 135
Do Not Lie 137
Change Versus Continuity 138
Thankful 2 141
Just Today 142
Rest 143
I Failed 145
Go The Distance 148
Blunt 150
Now 151
Nice Guys Finish Last 152
One Warrior 155
Donuts Or Do Nots 158
Break Away 160
I Will Fight 162
Justify 163
Ride Harder 166

Skill Set **167**
Not An Act, But A Habit 169
Week 1 172
IF/THEN 175
Perfect Practice Perfects Performance 178
Process 182
Natural Outcome 184
SOP 188
Slice the Gordian Knot 190
Play Ball 193
May I Ask You a Question? 194

vii

I Object	196
Win the Morning 2	200
One More	202
The Trichotomy of Control	204
Mutation	207
Continuous Improvement	211
Balance Daniel-San	213
Seduction	216
Tough Love	220
Psychology of Capitalism	222
The Trials of the Master	230
Independence	232
Fly	235
Centers	238
Multi-Channel Thought Processes and Cognitive Dissonance in Client Communication	242
Pain is a Barrier	246
Scout Camp	252
Hot	254
Thoughts on Thoughts	256
Scout Sale Story	260
Morning Joe	262
Small Things	264
Lab Rat	266
Passive Introductions	269
4th Quarter Hurry Up	272
APPENDIX	**273**

About the author

Joseph RR Templin has over two and a half decades of experience in financial services. He has numerous MDRT qualifications and has recruited over a hundred people into the profession. Joe was an Advisor Today 4 Under 40 Winner and has developed thousands of agents and Advisors, teaching them how to build vibrant and sustainable Introduction-Based Businesses ethically.

Even though he claims to be "more of a mathlete than an athlete," Joe has run multiple ultramarathons and is a former International Tae Kwon Do Champion. He is also a special needs parent and Cub Scout Packmaster. He is a die-hard Yankees fan and has three hooligan children.

Acknowledgements:

First and foremost, I want to thank my first Activity Coach, Carly Guy. She set me on the path of becoming an Introduction Machine, of getting paid every time I added value even if I never saw that person again or if they chose not to follow my recommendations for their future. That one conversation in 1995 was the lightning bolt, my satori moment that gave me my career and let me write this book to help you. Even though I haven't seen her in almost two decades, her impact will continue to ripple across the financial services landscape for decades. Carly, "Diamond Jim" Nemec, Bill Newman, and Ric Kelton were the earliest influences on me in my financial services career and demanded excellence. I'm glad they did.

Secondly, the man who has been a second father to me for decades, Master Danny Grant. It is he who pushed me, guided me, kicked my ass and made me better. He instilled professional pride as a martial artist, the mindset I transferred to my financial services career and beyond. The focus is on fundamentals, the practice of perfecting mindset, and the grit to overcome injuries or the unexpected. My oldest is named after him for a reason, and no matter what tournaments, titles, or accolades I achieve, I can never honor him sufficiently for what he has given me.

My Muse. You know who you are and why.

To my amigo Juan Ibarra for the kick in the pants to do this book, to bring these ideas out there in a book to reach more people and help them achieve their goals, people I will never personally meet. Thank you for the reminder of why we teach.

My Major Domo Athena for reminding me, "Bad stoic, no donut," and making sure I remember that I am a badass when I become weak, that I have a mission to make people better and pick them up when they are down, and that goes for myself.

My Tower of Power, Grant, reminds me that I deserve good things, that I don't have to love only the broken ones, and that we can all fix ourselves IF WE WANT TO and are willing to do the work.

Heidi. Because she still puts up with me and my antics.

And finally, to my dad, John Templin. His example of hard work, sacrifice for family, and what it meant to be a professional and a servant leader have given me a standard to uphold. I might not have followed his steps in healthcare consulting (sorry, Pop, I will always hate hospitals), but I think his legacy will have a more significant impact by exporting his lessons to other fields. He taught me to look for the pearls in everything, and I hope you find enough pearls in this book to make it a treasure and finance your dreams.

Background in Financial Services et al.

No Machine is perfect on the first iteration. Every system, be it mechanical, computer, or financial, requires tweaking to improve. The Intro Machine is no different. It still isn't close to optimized, but it is fully functional. We should look at how it evolved to understand some of the fundamentals of why it works.

"If I were giving a young man advice on how he might succeed, I would say to him, pick out a good father and mother and begin life in Ohio."

Wilbur Wright.

I didn't grow up in late 19th-century Ohio, but I was blessed to grow up in a small rural community. My hometown still has dirt roads, and we didn't have a traffic light until I was in Graduate School. It was on the main corner by the town hall and general store and blinked after 6:00 p.m. I can't make this stuff up.

So, being in a semi-farming community (and spending a lot of time on my Godfather's farm) with good parents, I learned many lessons that are easily translated into my professional endeavors. Some of these include:

1. Work Ethic
2. Stick-to-it-ness
3. Embracing The Cycle
4. Honor Your Word

We will not discuss the fourth of these much in this book because it is beyond the scope, and many other resources are available to help you in that space. We will hit on the first point throughout this book, sometimes subtly, other times like a brick through the window.

I finished my coursework for my Bachelor's in Physics at RPI (the oldest engineering school in the English-speaking world, where our sports teams are called "The Engineers," and the movie "Real Genius" was in many ways my life) a semester early and rolled right into graduate studies, working both as a Teaching Assistant and as a Research Assistant, which was a good lesson in hard work and financial hardship. It also continued to stoke my curiosity and capability to export concepts from one area to another, such as the concept of a musical phrase to a martial arts kata (pre-set forms) or resonance in a laser chamber to communication theory. I know, nerdy. However, the intellectual rigor from the lab and the experimentation mindset have allowed me to test every concept, and maxim presented to me later in financial services to find more efficient and effective approaches that work for me. You are obviously not me, but hopefully, some of the insight I have gleaned from tens of thousands of meetings can assist you in becoming an Introduction Machine.

I left the lab for various reasons, including the unexpected death of my Godfather, who did not have proper legal documentation or good advice. As such, we eventually lost the family farm. That's when I started working on an MBA, called the local Northwestern Mutual agency, and said, "I am coming to work for you." Yes, arrogance is something I struggled with and still do.

I was pushed over to Bill Newman, who was running the College Internship Program (this was before this program became a perennial Top 10 Internship in the country. Funny how after I joined, that happened). I got my license in the summer of 1995. I started as an Intern while working at a local store on the weekends, earning my second-degree black belt and training with an eye towards the Olympics, running the local college bar, and taking a full graduate load. It was good preparation for eventually doing Ultramarathons and working in startup companies.

Oh, and within six months, I ran our college internship program locally. My first taste was recruiting, training, and development in financial services. It's stuff I still love to this day.

We built a scratch agency, and I went full-time and was among the Top 10 former interns (Mike Gish Award) for all of NML, then Top 10 College Unit Director. I was making MDRT, writing 100+ lives a year, built a group health and an investment business (this is when insurance companies and investment firms first started to be able to do both), was heavily involved in NAIFA (National Association of Insurance and Financial Advisors), wrote Gen X focused articles (not on finance) for the local paper, kept training in martial arts, and got married. It was a whirlwind few years, including earning my CLU (when it was still ten courses), my ChFC, and passing the CFP® exam, all before I was 30. I recruited scores of financial Reps in addition to growing my own business and developing myself as a person, producer, and leader.

When it became apparent that I wouldn't be allowed to build my own office nor take over the one I had helped build (both of which had been proffered to me and I toiled towards for years), there was a mutual parting of the ways. I went out consulting, helping agencies and individuals with the knowledge I had acquired across the various dimensions. This led me to work with startups (a tale for another day), with a half dozen major insurance companies (some of which still use my innovations to help their newer agents become more productive), and write a lot more to try and capture my knowledge and share it to a broader audience.

At this point, I have recruited 120+ Reps into the profession (I still help recruit because this is the most incredible field in the world for the people with the right mindset, and the opportunities are better than ever, even with the regulatory environment being as helpful as ankle shackles in a marathon), done a million dollars of production in a year, been chosen as an Advisor Today 4 Under 40 Winner, and spoken all over the US and Canada in addition to having success as a writer.

I'm not a "pen and ink philosopher"; I have been there and done that, and I want to help show you the way because others have given me insight. Unlike other fields, we have a culture of sharing ideas in financial services simply because we will never write all the insurance or do all of the planning that needs to be done. We could all make the Million Dollar Round Table; still, more people would need our help, so embrace the growth and abundance mindset and let me help you help them.

Everything in this book is something others have taught me, or I figured out through research and trial and error. As I said, some of it might not resonate with you, and that's okay. As Bruce Lee says, *"Absorb what is useful, reject what is useless, and add what is essentially your own."* Build an Introduction Machine that works for you and your business instead of mindlessly copying mine.

Some Numbers

Remember that I am a baseball fan and a physicist, so I believe in the numbers. They can give us tremendous insight into what is going on (such as the spin rate on a curve ball or a breakdown in your closing ratio indicating a skill gap), the total effort (number of attempts to schedule appointments), and ultimately, success (lives written, premium, wins). The numbers are not the be-all and end-all (other than the Yankees having more titles than anybody else), but rather the stories they tell.

That said, here are three sets of numbers that I believe are critical for you to understand to be successful in Financial Services in the Roaring '20s.

1. **Your survival is Intricately Linked to the Number of Appointments Kept.**
2. **An Introduction is Valuable.**
3. **Americans Need You!**

Let's unpack the numbers that lead to these conclusions.

Survival is Intricately Linked to the Number of Appointments Kept.

This conclusion is based on the collected data I received looking at about fifteen years of recruiting and development in our General Agency of Northwestern Mutual, data that was shared with me in various recruiting and development meetings at the home office or other meetings, information gleaned from friends in leadership positions in different companies, and my research through Unique Minds Consulting Group. There are over 100,000 agents/Reps worth of data points, so we can accept the statistical validity of the information and agree with the conclusions.

Here is the kernel of truth: the number of weekly appointments you keep with clients determines your survival and ultimate success early in your career. Within 90 days of starting, the writing is on the wall.

Tier Zero: If you keep less than one appointment daily (5 per week), you should probably pack up. Your chances of survival are that number of kept per week. Seriously, are you even in business?

Now, I am a bit of a jerk. Ok, I am an intolerant jerk when it comes to laziness or people wasting the time of those who are trying to help them, which people in this category fall into almost always. Either spend an hour a day learning what I lay out in this book, pound the phone for two hours a day, and spend the next thirty days busting your butt like you are about to get fired (because you are, by the way), or pack up now and save everyone some heartache.

Suppose you are keeping less than one appointment per day (unless your average case size is $25,000+ or you inherited $ 100 million in assets to manage). In that case, you will go broke before you can build a critical mass of a client base, and your skill set isn't developing because you aren't doing it enough. People who have made it in the business with this level of early activity are outliers, and given the economics of the profession at this point, I doubt your management will tolerate keeping you around for very long if you aren't trying.

Tier One: 1-2 kept per day. Your chances of success are better, not just because you have more meetings but because of the skill set development. A Tier Two practitioner is gaining experience at twice the rate as a Tier One, and it takes at least 10 of any particular type of case to get the hang of it, so Tier Two is making their mistakes faster and getting to the point of understanding what they are doing with clients. The number of appointment times 1.5X is your chance, so if you keep eight meetings per week, you have a 12% chance of success. Your prescription for success is similar to Tier One: spend an hour practicing your language and pound the phones for 90 minutes daily. You can move into Tier Two in a month, but only through brute effort. It is 100% up to you to do the work to succeed.

Tier Two: 2-3 kept per day. So, 10-14 appointments per week. Your chance of success is about 2x your weekly kept. You don't need to be terrified; focus on consistently working on your skills (a few times per week minimum) and getting three appointments on the phone daily. Look at the average number of appointments you had scheduled per week over the past two months and focus on increasing that number by 2 for the next week (meaning you probably need to schedule 3-4 more a week to keep 2). You can move into Tier Three in a month with focused daily effort.

Tier Three: Three kept per day. This is a magic line. If you average three kept appointments per day, it is a coin flip whether you will make MDRT in the next few years and be in the business for the long term. But the odds are in your favor.

Practice your language and consistently call to set new appointments (at least two new ones daily). Focus on getting at least one Introduction in each meeting. A bit of attention will keep you consistently producing and growing your business.

Tier Four: 4 Kept per day or more. This is rarified air. If you get to this level, you have a 100% chance of making MDRT if you choose to stay in the industry (the only examples from our research that didn't either die or leave the industry for family reasons unrelated to production and have not yet reached critical client mass).

Suppose you have made it to Tier Three. In that case, you can get here by getting 2 Introductions per appointment, calling each day for at least two new appointments, and controlling your calendar because you can't schedule six or more appointments without discipline regarding when clients meet you. It's a good problem to have.

Remember, the number of appointments you keep is proportional to the number of appointments you have set (typically a 60% kept rate for newer Reps, approaching 75% for established ones). The number of appointments you have set is 100% under your control.

Your survival is not dependent upon who is in the White House, the weather, or anything other than your efforts. If you accept this and take ownership of your career and work, you will succeed.

An Introduction is Valuable.

I get paid in Introductions, whether a client cuts me a check for planning fees or buys products. I get paid with Introductions every time because every Introduction is worth, on average, over $100.

Don't believe me? Let's do some math. We will use a forward projection for a new advisor rather than an established one. If you have been in the business for longer than a quarter, you can do the same calculation with your activity and production numbers.

Let's assume you make $50,000 for the year if you got 500 Introductions (10 a week for 50 weeks total, or 2 per day, a typical number for new Reps that have not yet bought into the value of Introductions).

$50,000/500 per Intro = $100 per Intro It's pretty simple, and it's about what I have seen on average for relatively new Agents and Advisors. As I said, if you have your numbers, you should calculate the value of an Introduction so that you buy into what I am discussing here even more.

Does this mean you get four Introductions today and $400 on Friday? Of course not. One, this is an average. Roughly one out of ten Introductions becomes a client, and there is a lag time of typically six to ten weeks from getting the Introduction to getting paid. NB: this time horizon has stretched out with COVID-19 partially because of the massive uptick in insurance applications and the disruptions to everything from getting medicals performed to getting paperwork through underwriting. If you continuously get 2 Introductions per meeting, your cash flows will stabilize because you have filled your sales pipeline, and things will progress naturally. Trust the process.

So, are you leaving C Notes on the table? If you do not ask whenever you sit down with someone and create value, you leave a handful of Benjamins on the table.

If every Introduction is worth $100 towards your compensation, getting TWO more a week translates into a $10,000-a-year raise. What would your friends in other fields do for ten thousand dollars? All you have to do is ask one more person a week who else you should talk to to see if you can help them. That simple.

Americans Need You!

Ok, let us look at some demographics and data.

Only about 20% of Americans own individual disability insurance. That means that 80% of the working population is at financial risk if they get hurt or injured. Workers' Compensation doesn't cover this, nor does Social Security.

Per LIMRA, 40+ million Americans say they need/want life insurance but don't have it. And how Many need more than what they have.

Millennials (the largest group in America, born between 1980 and 1997) overwhelmingly want guaranteed income for their retirement. Can you say "annuities"? Zoomers (1997 to 2012) even more so.

Over a third of Zoomers want to start a business (portability of benefits), and they save at a higher rate than any of the previous four generations.

Three out of four people reaching 65 (the Baby Boomers) will need long-term care at some point.

The average new college graduate spends more time planning their Spring Break trip than their financial future. They are functionally illiterate about budgeting, taxes, retirement plans, health insurance, legal documents, disability, and life insurance. They crave unbiased guidance and a social, professional relationship with an Advisor.

There is more student loan debt than mortgage debt in the US.

The Federal Reserve says the average American cannot handle a $400 unexpected expense.

According to the Congressional Budget Office, income taxes will have to go up by over 50% to cover the Federal Government's obligations BEFORE COVID-19 hits.

The Federal Deficit will hit $50T in a decade.

The Silent Generation (people born before the end of WWII but too young to fight it), the Greatest Generation (those who fought in WWII), and the older Boomers will pass more wealth than at any other time in history over the next twenty years, somewhere around $35 TRILLION.

Given these facts, can you think of even a single person in the US who doesn't need the financial products that you have within your arsenal?

Add to this the uncertainty about taxes and Social Security and how to pay for college or pay down individual debt, the lack of short-term and long-term savings, turnover in the job market, general anxiety, miscommunication, and misconceptions about money (a leading cause of divorce). You have roughly 300 million potential clients.

Don't tell me you have no one to talk to.

Everyone is waiting for an introduction to happen.

Process

OK, remember that I went to an engineering school (Hell, they are called the Rensselaer Engineers. Watch out, or we will disintegrate you!), so I have had the following processes beaten into me for thirty years.

The following processes were something that I have been accustomed to for even longer. Not only did my father also go to dear old Rensselaer (the college of our hearts!), but he was an Army officer, so SOP (Standard Operating Procedures) have been well SOP since I was a kid. I didn't know what it was called; it was more "do as you're told" or "the best way to get stuff done." Later, I learned about Henry Ford and his assembly line, Taylor, and efficiency methodologies. I just knew that because of my ADHD, I needed to do things the same way and check the boxes to make sure I didn't miss anything with everything I had going on.

One of my mentors, Ric Kelton (who is even more driven and crazier than I am), came from Arthur Anderson Consulting into financial services. Hence, he first looked at every action, from the phone calls to setting up appointments to client contact to the sales cycle, to ensure we had a consistent process. I glommed onto this and added efficiency and psychology onto everything we did to create a process from initial contact through the entire planning cycle and ongoing service that still has me in contact with clients twenty-five plus years later and generates consistent opportunities for me to be introduced to new potential clients at essentially every step.

As I repeatedly tell new Reps, **process over product**. A client might not be ready to buy whatever policy strategy or tool. Still, the process will ensure the highest quality of guidance for them and that they get more value from working with me than expected while being easy for my team to run. This maximizes the chances that they will buy something and earn any planning fees. Even if the potential client does not work with us, they walk away respecting my organization and are more often than not an advocate, sometimes returning to us over time to work with us when the time is right for them.

The process is more powerful than the people running it.

If you have never read Michael Gerber's "The E Myth Revisited," I highly suggest doing so. As he says, it doesn't matter if you are a poodle groomer or a neurosurgeon; you need to have every step of the process documented so the lowest possible appropriately skilled person can run the systems. Thus, instead of requiring the rockstar and overpaying for the uniquely qualified person to assist you in building and running your financial services machine (that takes in Introductions and spits out clients and money), you can have someone proficient in Microsoft Office who has passed their licensing exams, is hardworking, and follows directions. You don't need to hire an expert because the process just needs to be run to achieve results.

The Sales Cycle:

The Sales Cycle (the iterative process I use to work with financial planning clients) is too long. The process has too many micro steps to go through in this book (see Choices: Creating a Financial Services Career by Stolk and Templin for an in-depth discussion). Most importantly, The Sales Cycle is a process, and you can't cut corners. If a new person comes into your office and says, "My attorney says I need to buy $10,000,000 of life insurance to go into a trust for my estate planning." Then, by all means, set up the medical and start that application process. However, you still need to explain how you do business, ask the basic questions, review the documents, discuss with the attorney, and do paperwork and underwriting. Follow your process to ensure you don't miss anything and deliver the same high-quality service you always do, not just taking an order and saying, "Would you like fries with that, too?"

Cutting corners creates chaos—and potential lawsuits.

General Sales Cycle Steps:

1. **Setup Appointment**
2. **Process and Payment Discussion**
3. **Data Gathering**
4. **Education**
5. **Solution Presentation**
6. **Implementation**
7. **Service**

Your firm may use a very different vocabulary than I just laid out. Still, I want the steps to be generic enough that anyone from a warehouse to an insurance company to a credit union can understand them.

Setup Appointment. When I entered the business, this was called "dialing for dollars," I picked up the phone and called people (either referrals or cold calls; the Powers That Be didn't care as long as your appointment book was full). I don't care how you set up your appointments, as long as you consistently get enough of them to run the sales activity you need to succeed. If you are not running the activity you need to and are not doing at least a few of the following, you might want to supplement what you are doing to have a full calendar and hit your production goals.

1. Dialing. The old pick up the phone and call potential clients.
2. Texting. Effective for reaching Gen X.
3. DM. If you don't know, this means Direct Messaging on various social media platforms, so stick with 1, 2, 4, and 5.
4. Email.
5. Face to Face. Like knocking on a door or having someone personally introduce you at a party, in the office, or at an event.

Ensure you have a way for people to schedule with you (such as a calendar link in your emails and your website). People are lazy, so make it easy for them.

PROCESS

The goal of setting up the appointment is to set up the appointment. Don't try to sell them on some fantastic product or idea, don't try to make them think you are the greatest thing since the internet, and do not try to get Introductions at this point. This is one of the only times I will say that: do not try to get Intros! Patience, Daniel-San!

Process and Payment Discussion. This is a specific step because it is critical to establishing the relationship with the client and ensuring they become part of your marketing team. I see new Financial Reps skip this all the time, and then they wonder why the people they talk with get squirrely and buy their products elsewhere or, worse, don't give Introductions to keep feeding the machine.

The first part of this component is explaining your process to the client. They want to know who you are, what you do for them, and how you will do it. I don't care if you use something simple like saying you do offensive (accumulation strategies) and defensive (insurance and tax planning) or go into a four-phase iterative diagram with badly drawn pictures as I do. The important thing here is that the client understands what you do (as well as they can upfront) and the steps to minimize surprises.

The second part of this step is the Payment Discussion. Clients get upset when they feel a lack of transparency, so they need to know how you get paid upfront. Commissions? Tell them that. Planning fees and/or assets under management fees? Tell them. You probably have some documentation to give them, so do so.

But more important than the cash compensation (not to the regulators, but to you and your Introduction-Based Business that you are building) is the verbal contract of them buying into you and your team, about them believing in your value.

If you took computer programming, you would understand "Boolean Logic." If you took any form of basic logic or philosophy, you'd recognize the concept of a conditional contract, an "if... then" statement. The last part of your **Payment Discussion** needs to be an agreement with the potential client that regardless of whether they buy something or pay you a fee, or not if they find the time spent with you valuable, they will introduce you to other people who could benefit from a similar discussion.

"**If** Mr. or Miss Potential Client, at the end of our meeting today, you can say, "Wow, you opened my eyes and helped me." whether it is giving you more insight into what you should do for retirement, reducing your tax bill, clarifying your budget, or helping you understand why you make the financial decisions you do, **if** at the end of our discussion today you can say that I helped you, **then** I ask that you introduce me to other people that could benefit from a similar conversation. Is that fair and reasonable?" Something along these lines is what I ALWAYS say when I sit down with a new potential client to get their verbal handshake right at the start. So that they know I would ask for Introductions if I earned the right to request one, and it's not a surprise.

At this point, you might have to answer a couple of objections, which are easy to neutralize as long as you stay calm and follow The Pirate Model of handling objections that we will introduce later. Of the 7,500+ initial meetings I have had, precisely TWO times someone said they wouldn't introduce me to others if I helped them. I chose to work with neither of those people because I like getting paid for my time.

Every Introduction is a payment in my mind, a lottery ticket with a 10% chance of paying me

$1,000+. If you looked at Introductions that way, you'd get ten a day if possible, and you can do so by following the process we are laying out throughout this book.

Note that at the end of every meeting, you can ask for additional Introductions **if** you have added value in that meeting. You should always add value to every single meeting with a client. Otherwise, you are wasting their time. The language I use at the end of each session is simple and straightforward: Mr. Client, what was the most valuable thing we discussed today? Then I shut up, let them convince themselves how valuable the meeting was to them, and then say, "As we agreed when we first sat down, if I added value, you would introduce me to other people I could potentially help. With that in mind..." And I make it easy for them to then think of high-quality people for me to talk to (more on this later).

Data Gathering. Your company probably has an intake form that you should use. Add to that what you learn from more experienced representatives and from attending professional association meetings like NAIFA, Finseca, or Estate Planning Council. Get the technical and psychological information, the feelings that underlay what it says on the financial statements. The more connected you become with the client, the more likely you will get high-quality Introductions.

Education. This is a great chance to add value because you can teach clients things they didn't know. Show them alternatives to save for retirement or college beyond what they are doing, do a gap analysis on their insurance programs, and point out if they have missing legal documents. This is where you should be more professional than a salesperson and truly differentiate yourself from the stereotypes.

Solution Presentation. Or as they used to say, "Closing". You ask for the business.

Implementation. Paperwork is the bane of salespeople everywhere. Then, underwriting and then getting everything put in force. Tediousness requires attention to detail, which is probably among the things you love the most (not!). But still, it is a chance to shepherd the client through the byzantine path and earn points with them that you can collect for additional Introductions.

Trust me, get the staff to do this as soon as possible.

Service. Look, it's called "Financial Services" for a reason. More than address changes, there are constant changes in the tax code, family situations, the economy, and everything else. Your job is to make sure your clients worry as little as possible and communicate with them so that they know you are on top of it and can focus on their family, business, life, etc.

I used to have clients come in for reviews with typed lists of people for me to call, saying, "We only have four here; we'll think of someone before we are finished today." That is what superior effort throughout the Sales Cycle yields.

As a rule, you should average two introductions per meeting, whether the first time you sit down with a client or the fifteenth. If you stick to your process, use the proper if/then statements, and focus on adding value to your clients every single time, this will be the natural output from the process.

Now that you understand the sales cycle let's look at some processes that you should incorporate to increase your value for the client and create more perceived value for yourself.

1. Check List of Documents/Information
2. Agendas
3. Synopsis Letter
4. Standardization of Presentations

As you work on your business, you should eventually make everything you do a process that can be iteratively run, as much as possible, by staff members so that you can focus on the highest and best use (stealing the IRS term) of your time: being face to face with clients building relationships, solving problems, and getting introduced to other people. Everything else can be delegated.

I will include my checklists for Documents/Information in the Appendix, copies of Agendas for various types of meetings, and feeder list examples. Feel free to steal and modify them to fit your needs; make sure your Sales Prevention Department (oops, I mean "Compliance Department") reviews and signs off on you using them so I don't have managers with pitchforks and torches coming after me.

Now, a word on standardized presentations. This doesn't mean cookie-cutter, where everyone gets the same thing.

Every TYPE of client receives the same PAGES and the same analysis with individual data and goals. Mass customization and assembly line analysis allow you to master your presentations so you know exactly what page comes next and can focus on the client instead of the analysis. I have used these presentations for my first decade, so you have an idea. I would present the modules in parentheses; each had the same page and was personalized to the client and their situation.

1. Single No Kids (Introduction, Financial Concepts, Disability, Death, Retirement,

Recommendations)

2. Married No Kids (Introduction, Financial Concepts, Disability, Death, Retirement, Recommendations)
3. Single Kids (Introduction, Financial Concepts, Disability, Death, College, Retirement, Recommendations)
4. Married Kids (Introduction, Financial Concepts, Disability, Death, College, Retirement, Recommendations)
5. Married Empty Nesters (Introduction, Financial Concepts, Disability, Death, College, Long Term Care, Retirement, Estate Planning, Recommendations)
6. Widowed Empty Nester (Introduction, Financial Concepts, Disability, Death, College, Long Term Care, Retirement, Estate Planning, Recommendations)

I would remove modules as appropriate, making it easier for my staff and myself. There is a reason I could keep 18+ Personal Planning appointments per week, plus 5+

Management ones, and still be at my martial arts class at 6:00 every night. And no weekend meetings.

Systems allow you to scale.

Processes lead to productivity.

The Process of Asking for Introductions

The first thing about having a process is that it's not a sometimes thing. It's an everyday thing. I ask for introductions when I sit with a client and add value. Long-term clients laugh about it because I am so consistent with it, and they know how important it is to the longevity of my business.

I used to have young computer coders or engineers tell me, "Joe, you already work with everyone in my office. Every. Last. One." To which I'd respond: Awesome, who do you still talk to that you went to school with? That you like and respect?" They'd laugh, I'd laugh, I'd get more Introductions, and everyone won.

But seriously, I can't understate the importance of consistency. Talking about Introductions has to be a constant thing, partially because you are conditioning your brain the same way an athlete conditions their body or a musician masters their craft. We all have internal programming in our brain (called the Reticular Activation System or RAS), the filter through which we see the world. You can make yourself see the opportunities for Introductions, the way a serial entrepreneur considers the opportunities to build new businesses, or a writer sees the inspiration for poems in everyday situations.

All skills require practice, and the ability to uncover and harvest introductions is no different. Every professional athlete practices like it's their job because, quite frankly, it is.

It is your job to hone your skills so that every time you have an opportunity to ask for Introductions (which is every time you add value, which should be every time you interact. with a client) you do so. From this point forward, we will assume that you are practicing your language regularly so that you don't have to think about what to say to your client; you do it because you have practiced it to the point that you are unconsciously competent.

How much practice is that? I had a fish in my office, and every morning, I would practice my language on it. It would give me objections such as "I can't think of anyone" or "Let me talk to them first," and I practiced how to deal with any objection (my Pirate Model works well) each morning. Other people in my office would make fun of me, but they were usually out of the business within a few months because they didn't practice and hone their craft like I did.

So, the straightforward steps in my process for getting Introductions were:

1. Tell them you are going to ask.
2. Earn the right to ask.
3. Ask.
4. Make it easy.

It is so simple that even a Red Sox fan can understand it, but for them, I will repeat it because it is so important.

1. Tell them you are going to ask.
2. Earn the right to ask.
3. Ask.

4. Make it easy.

We discussed the first step (Tell them you will ask) in the Sales Cycle Payment Discussion component. This is critical because, as I said, I create a verbal contract with them (the Deal Before the Deal as it is sometimes called. If you have studied the Sandler Sales Method, you recognize this), where I get their word as a person of integrity that they will pay me (with Introductions) if and when I create value. It is hard to reach Step 2 if you skip Step 1. That applies everywhere, by the way.

Now, Step 2 is the hardest part. Earn the right to ask.

Create value.

Help them.

One exercise you should do is take a piece of paper and write across the top of it, "Ways I Create Value." Then, start writing how you create value for a client. And don't say, "Sell them Life Insurance," as it's a commodity in the client's mind, and there are over half a million people they could buy it from, plus go online and order it. Nor should you say something high fallutin' like "I give structure to people's financial situation," because would your grandmother or a teenager understand what that means? Thought not. Forget the buzzwords and look beyond the ubiquitous products.

To help you, here is a list of ways I create value. Use it as a starter, then add to it your spin (remember, you're not me. You're probably better looking, less goofy, and not as fascinated with esoteric information as I am. Be the best YOU possible, not an evil clone of me.).

I Create Value:

1. When I get a client to create a budget.
2. When I get a client to have a plan for paying down debt.
3. When I educate a client on what a Human Life Value is.
4. When I find shortfalls in their disability insurance coverage.
5. When I make a client check their beneficiary designations.
6. When I get a client to get their legal documents updated.
7. When I show clients that maxing out their 401k creates a future tax issue.
8. When I get a couple to openly discuss their feelings about money.
9. If I can get a client to contribute to their work retirement plan.
10. When a client builds an emergency fund.
11. If I make a client review their liability coverage.
12. If I prevent a client from making a million-dollar mistake.
13. If my client can sleep better at night.
14. If I introduce my client to another professional to help them.
15. Whenever I educate my client. Now it is your turn.

I create value by: 1. 2. 3. 4. 5. 6. 7. 8. 9. 10.

My primary focus whenever I meet with clients is to create value for them. Why are they coming to see me if I am not creating value? If we are going to work on our relationship,

I'd rather go to the pub (and admit it, they'd rather sit down outside the office with an adult beverage of some form, too). And if I don't create value, I don't deserve any Introductions.

Because I didn't earn them, it allows my mental focus to shift from me and what I want to the client and improve their world, helping them reach their goals (financial or otherwise).

As the Rotarians say, givers get. Give them what they need, and you'll get the Introductions that you need.

Will Set

Everyone is looking for the silver bullet to build their business, the magic sales technique that will result in all the people you want to talk to calling you and allowing you to sit back and watch the production roll in.

Sorry, buttercup, it's not happening. All good things come from work. Hard work.

Look, it is going to suck. And if you are focusing on building an Introduction Based Business (IBB), it is going to suck every day. If you aren't ready to quit at least once a day, then you aren't pushing yourself (or you're a freak. And if that is the case, then keep pushing harder until you get to that place where you are ready to quit and back off one iota because that is an epic level right there.). People make money (real money) because they either do stuff that others can't do (hit both a 99-mph fastball and the curve) or they do things others won't do (garbage collectors, oil rig workers, etc.). Building a financial services business is a combo of the two, and you should be able to be in the top 10% of earners in your area within 18 months of reading (and applying) this book. Not because of the magical language and Jedi Mind Tricks, but because of your mental toughness and willingness to fail over and over because you are still piling up enough wins (even if negligible to begin with) to, as Dr. Jordan Peterson proclaims, *"justify your suffering."* Pain with a purpose: to get better and to build the business and life you want.

But you have to want it. Not "Oh, that would be nice to have," but a "I gotta do this, succeeding is more important than anything, and I don't care about embarrassing myself or having someone hang up on me or get pissed at me." You need to want to win (the long game, not necessarily each meeting) more than anything else because it will give you EVERYTHING else.

Will Set is stick-to-it-ness. The burning fire produces champions by melting away all the rubbish, burning away what is dead or useless in us. And that fire comes from an inner spark you feed into a flame.

It is the absolute belief that you were put on this earth to do this and that you are ready to tell the potential client what they need to hear (not what they want to hear) because you are on a mission from God (to quote the Blues Brothers) to help them reach their best future. THAT is the attitude you need to have.

And it's not a beating-the-chest, screaming alpha male thing. I know powerful, soft-spoken women who produce over half a million dollars a year and are made of steel inside because they believe in what they are doing.

Sales is ultimately a transfer of belief systems between people, and whoever has the most robust belief system can sway the other and get the outcome they seek. As Friederich Nietzsche proclaimed, *he who has a strong enough why can bear almost any how.* So go back and review WHY you want to do this, buy into that reason with all of your being, and then read these pages to reinforce and reinvigorate yourself for the hard work needed to win your particular prize.

Activation Energy

I talked with one of my nerd buddies the other morning, and she brought up the idea of activation energy. Since most people reading this haven't taken a chemistry class this millennium, let's review: Arrhenius postulated over a hundred and twenty-five years ago that it takes an influx of energy to get a reaction going. Essentially, a chemical reaction needs a jump start, like you have that coffee in the morning to get going, and then you are functional. For a good article (where I stole the diagram), checkout Activation Energy: Why Getting Started Is the Hardest Part (fs. blog)

The reaction after getting over the hump can then keep going. Like pushing a boulder up a little ridge and then crashing down into the valley below to take out the enemy (an example of gravitational potential energy being converted into kinetic energy), chemical potential energy needs a little bit of influx to unleash what it has stored up like seed capital for a start-up firm that then explodes or investing money into a marketing plan that takes a few weeks to get going but then is cash-flow positive and self-sustaining.

When building an Introduction Business, there is an upfront energy investment in a few parts of the equation. The first is entirely mental and involves you buying into the idea that getting paid with Introductions every time you create value is how you will build your business. I was talking with a very successful businessman whose business has fallen off recently, and he told me that he only asks for introductions from someone who buys. I pointed out that means he is only asking about one in four of the people he is meeting with, and that is the reason his activity is low now and spiraling down because he is less effective closing due to scarcity mentality restricting his capabilities combined with a shrinking pool of prospects. If you create value for a client, you earn the right to ask for Introductions and can get paid many more times than if you only ask those who buy. Getting this individual to overcome his inertia requires mental effort and is the influx of activation energy needed to start the process.

There is a secondary energy hump, though: the relationship with the individual you are talking with. You will have to invest in them to get something out of them. You are going to have to lay out the parameters of the professional relationship and the exchange of value, you are going have to take the time and mental energy to understand them and assist them, and then you are going to have to take the emotional risk of rejection to ask for your introductions. You have to work. But you can also get them over the introduction threshold by making it easy for them to introduce you when you ask. One way is to feed them back a name from your discussion ("earlier you had mentioned so and so. Tell me a little about them") or ask for someone particular ("I usually talk with my client's attorney, who is yours?"), or have a list of names and categories ready to go. All work is done to get the client over the activation energy required to introduce you. Then, the additional introductions beyond the first flow are more accessible and easier to use in a sustainable reaction.

If you were to think about it, the idea that you have to give to get is not outlandish. Science for the win again! So, make the upfront investment of energy in yourself and your clients to overcome the activation energy, get over the hump, and see what the reaction is.

Discipline

Former Navy SEAL Jocko Willink speaks the brutal but beautiful and ugly truth about war, leadership, and excellence, not just in execution for battle or training but in life. And he restates something drilled into me as a new financial Rep two and a half decades ago: discipline equals freedom.

Vince Lombardi proclaimed: *Winning is a Habit.*

Aristotle taught that *"We are what we repeatedly do. Excellence, therefore, is not an act, but a habit."*

As a new Rep, we were repeatedly taught, "To live like a king, you need to live like a slave."

Og Mandino preached, *"I will form good habits and become their slave."*

We have seen new Reps fail repeatedly because they don't have enough qualified people to call. This is one area of their practice that is almost entirely under their control, so failure to acquire enough referrals to run their machine is 100% on them.

There is one tiny thing that these rookies can do to change their outcome. It's simple but not easy.

Most importantly, it takes discipline.

It takes discipline to do their prep work before every encounter in the field.

It takes discipline to practice their craft every single day.

It takes discipline to ASK for introductions every single time.

It would be easier to sit on the couch and veg out at night or watch Game of Thrones than to run feeder lists for your meetings. But who says you can't do both at the same time?

It would be easier not to say, "Let's pause and take a minute to brainstorm here..." and let the client get away with saying, "I can't think of anyone," instead of engaging, challenging, and guiding them to answers.

In fact, almost ANYTHING is easier than looking a person in the eye and asking for the introductions you deserve for helping this person because of our ego. We fear rejection.

We are afraid of being told "no."

Our egos do not want to be exposed to the risk of another person essentially saying, "I don't like you enough to introduce you to another person."

And so, we weasel out of asking because it is uncomfortable. Thus discipline.

It hurts to get rejected.

Lifting weights, running the hill, or getting hit while practicing a sport hurts. And yet you did it.

You practiced and improved.

You scrimmaged and implemented what you practiced. You played the game and played to win.

You didn't win every time, but you gave it your all every time. Because of the discipline you developed.

Why is your career, your future, and the future of others less important than a game? Take the shot.

Ask the questions for introductions every time.

Practice asking the questions so you don't think when it is game time. Then, you can execute your game plan with the skills that are ingrained in you at a subconscious level from practice.

From discipline.

The Master has failed more times than the beginner has ever tried.

Because they have decades of discipline, but all Masters were neophytes once. And they developed the habits of practice, of discipline.

Because Discipline equals Freedom.

Training the Will

Ever have a goal that motivates you to get up early and bust your butt before the sunrises to chase it down? Maybe it was running that marathon or graduate school or that licensing exam that made you get out of bed at o-dark thirty, over and over and over again. Or maybe it was so big that you couldn't tell anyone because they'd think you were crazy.

> "Here's to the crazy ones. The misfits. The rebels. The troublemakers. The round pegs in the square holes. The ones who see things differently. They're not fond of rules. And they have no respect for the status quo... Because the people who are crazy enough to think they can change the world, are the ones who do."
> Steve Jobs

I've been doing that for years; everyone knows some of what I've been working on, but for once, I've kept my mouth shut (no comments).

The Intro Machine was initially created to help agents and advisors (primarily the younger ones raised in the social media world) use technology to enhance their capabilities and get introductions (referrals) regularly. But we quickly realized that a tool without training is pretty useless and that there were significant voids in the mindset and development of those we were trying to help, specifically in two areas: Skill Set and Will Set.

I will return to address Skill Set later, but Will Set is fundamental and an attitude that goes well beyond business and deserves primary attention, for where there is a will, there shall be a way.

I recently ran an ultramarathon (100km in a day), which was much easier than the double marathon (52.5 miles) I had done six months before. The main difference was between my ears, partly because of a better understanding of nutritional needs and maybe a little because of better physical preparation. And in my guts, because Will is what it takes to go beyond the commonly accepted limits.

Why was my Will so much better this time around? Partially because I was almost destroyed the first time, where after 40 miles, I was on pure fumes, and my nearly empty emotional tank unexpectedly was drained to help another. This forced me to find strengths within myself I didn't comprehend that I had, which I then knew were there for this much longer run only six months later.

Pushing yourself to your limits and beyond is the best way to discover who you are and what you are capable of. It makes you understand that you are more than what you have previously accomplished, much more than you show the world (and yourself) on a regular basis. Going to extremes raises your norms and what you will accept from yourself if you decide to operate at the elite level you have reached.

Look, I'm not a fast runner by any measurement. But I do it and keep doing it. Maybe you're not an elite work performer gifted with sheer raw talent. But you can work and improve your standards and maximize the potential you have. Everyone argues over what percent of our brain potential we use (10%, 20%?), but it is still far from 100%, so we can do more mentally and physically than we usually achieve. The difference between a Master and an Apprentice is not talent but effort applied over years and decades. Who cares what your full potential is, as none of us will reach it? Just focus on doing what it takes to be better this week than last, and keep going and growing for as long as you can!

So, push those limits, and they expand a little. It doesn't matter if you are stretching from running a mile to running a mile and a quarter, then 1.5, then two miles. Or do more pushups or do anything you are currently incapable of. Do the work and push yourself to get better over and over and over, and you'll eventually be good or even great. And that takes not Skill but Will to suck at something and grind to improve, again and again and again.

To do that workout.

To crack those books.

To sit down and write for an hour or more every morning, day after day, for six months.

And not just an hour in the morning but at lunch, after work, and before bed.

Do the work. Your skills will improve, but the effort to do what you know you should (be it in that relationship, for that degree, or on that project) is what builds your will daily so that you can test it in a massive effort like a marathon or exam or life itself.

And that is why I am pleased to announce my subsequent oeuvre to assist you: "Every Day Excellence: A Daily Guide to

Growing." This daily training book is designed to help grow your Will Set across multiple dimensions (fitness, discipline, relationships, spirituality, health, etc.) every single day so that you can tap into your greatness. Every Day Excellence is the outcome of a thousand hours of work over six months of getting up early and staying up late, of sacrifice and soul-draining effort to help you look at what you are doing and becoming and improve it.

Stay tuned for more details, but remember: a marathon is a massive accomplishment, but it is composed of small steps put together in a way that tests and reveals your true power. This book is a more concrete example of mine and will help you unlock yours.

This is Going to Suck

The other day, it was overcast and approaching dusk. The wind started picking up, and I looked at the weather report. Wind, sleet, rain. I decided to go for a run with the thought, "Well, this is going to suck!"

I purposely chose to put myself in an uncomfortable position—cold, wet, hungry, and miserable—so that I could become better.

I chose to be in a situation that would stress me out and make me have to reach into my core and succeed sheerly on my gut. Every squishy step, every gust that cut through me on that short but nasty four kilometers, the drops falling off the brim of my hat as my gloves soaked in the rain and became heavy and frigid, each moment forced me to tap into my reserves.

By drawing on the deposits of grit I had developed, I set aside more for the future, for the next time I have to dig deep. It could be my ultramarathon; it could be in the office or my relationships. Facing pain and weakness, pushing to the point of vulnerability and beyond the normal limits expands those limits and makes us stronger overall for ourselves and others.

What can you do this week that you will look at and say, "Well, this is going to suck," and then do it anyway, knowing that the pain is temporary, but the character developed is eternal?

Burn

I would rather spectacularly fail at a glorious and worthy endeavor than lie, shirk, or turn tail and be doomed to Darkness forever. It is better to burn with Passion and Light than to be Void and fade into the Night.

No Pill

There is no pill.

There is no silver bullet or magic potion.

Want to lose weight? Eat less and exercise more. It is about caloric deficit, which means expending more energy than you consume. Change what you eat and increase your activity levels. If you are not a hundred-plus kilograms overweight, radical surgeries and the like are unnecessary; some discipline and compounding small changes are—no overnight miracles, but significant changes and improvements over time.

Want to increase your production and build a successful business? There are no Harry Potteresque magic words or alien technology to move the pieces into place. You are going to have to work at it. More hours, or better yet more effective, like the difference between modern machinery and putting logs under heavy stones and pulling with animals. More innovative work, but you are still going to have to work. You need to learn to operate the machines; it still takes time and dirty, messy work to build something worthwhile. Rome was not built in a day, as the saying goes.

Everyone wants to go to Heaven, but no one wants to die the Marines intone. They also say that pain is weakness leaving the body, and it doesn't leave in a nice comfy sauna with sandalwood and herb scents and a fluffy robe. It is sweated out through intense work on all levels. You will have to work, and it will take time to improve and convert weaknesses into strengths. Celebrating and pampering yourself is not bad, but if you don't go through boot camp and fight in the trenches, often you can't truly appreciate the nice things because they aren't earned; they are a distraction from emptiness instead of a reward for accomplishments and well-earned rewards. The most lavish celebrations happen after the hardest-fought victories.

Make the little hard choices. Call that client that scares you. Ask people for Introductions. Sacrifice the time to study your craft and practice your vocabulary. Trade time for excellence now so you can have more time and rewards in the future.

There is no pot of gold just because you want easy riches. There is, however, a gold mine, and there are tools to help you get to work. Pick them up and dig beneath the surface, break a sweat to break through to where the precious material lays waiting because others won't do the work, so they can't get the rewards that go to those willing to bust their hump over time.

If success comes easily, it can disappear as quickly as possible. But the process of becoming a champion leaves marks on your soul. The imprint of hard work, discipline, and sacrifice echoed over the years. Awaken the echoes of excellence.

As Nobel Peace Prize and Congressional Medal of Honor Winner Teddy Roosevelt proclaimed: *"Nothing in the world is worth having or worth doing unless it means effort, pain, difficulty... I have never envied a human being who led an **easy** life."* Choose the more challenging path, the more difficult choices, and earn a life of envy. That might be a bitter pill, but you are on the path to glory once you do.

Passion as Fuel

Distress kills. Eustress empowers. Harness the positive aspect of stress to fuel your journey to excellence.

What is Eustress? Tim Ferriss popularized the phrase in his New York Times Bestseller "The 4-Hour Work Week" as a descriptor for the positive aspects of stress that energize and invigorate your competitive juices. Yet it was initially published in Nature in 1936 by a Canadian biochemist and has been overshadowed by the negative aspect of Stress for eighty years. Anyone who has been an athlete or performs music or theatre knows the feeling of rising to the challenge of a rival, giving your all, and feeling remarkable about the process of becoming great regardless of the outcome. Those who embrace eustress eventually become champions because they fall in love with the work of becoming great instead of the accolades, as Schwarzenegger proclaims.

Find what is not work but fun in its purest form that makes you want to develop mastery and work so hard that you forget to eat and tear yourself away to force yourself to sleep. Watch a 12-year-old playing Fortnight and care deeply about your work. Have an outlet to positively channel your fight or flight in alignment with your goals, and work becomes play.

You can call it "Flow," as Csikszentmihalyi does in his book of the same name. Still, eustress leads to flow in that it builds the fundamental strengths needed to create that innate desire to rise up, become great, and achieve mastery over an area or subject, whether skateboarding or martial arts or building an Introduction-based Business. Eustress raises your energy levels (as opposed to distress that lowers them), and, in the end, you say, "I'm tired, but it's a good sort of tired!"

Contrast this with the effects of distress, which produce cortisol in the body, leading to inflammation and damage. Christopher Bergland discusses this idea in a 2013 article. This also decreases testosterone levels, thus reducing peak energy levels and stamina. Negative stress weakens the body and, over time, can lead to breakdowns from the cellular level to the muscular and even mental. Injecting eustress into typically distressful situations will lead to better time management, workflow, and emotions and shorter recovery times between significant endeavors.

One way to flip stress to eustress is the concept of gamification. In this, you are making a game out of something serious, and the results can be pretty spectacular if done correctly. Several of the biggest insurance companies use little ribbons to denote production levels at their meetings, and the amount of additional effort a big producer will exert to get a tiny scrap of cloth is a wonder of performance psychology. The educational world realized a while ago that children learn through play, and there are thousands of programs such as these learning games in a classroom setting. Every library has a summer reading contest with prizes to harness this concept and convert it into a desire to read and learn, something corporate America has been too slow to adopt.

Make a game out of getting introductions. Set a daily goal that will translate (based on your sales ratios) to hitting your monthly production goals. Now, round it up to the following whole number, and that is your Daily Intro Goal (DIG).

Now, create a game that works for you to achieve your DIG consistently. Examples we have used in the past include:

1. Hit your DIG daily and put a penny in a small stack by your phone. When you get five pennies, you get to do something small, like buy a nice bottle of wine or a six-pack of good beer or go to the movies. These are appropriate little rewards for hitting your goal every day for a week.

2. Thermometer: Every day you hit your DIG, you fill in a little thermometer, and when you hit a specific temperature (say 32 degrees for 32 days), you get a good reward, like new shoes or a tie.

3. Marble jar: a marble per day of hitting your DIG. When the jar is full, you get to do a night out or take the kids to the amusement park. You can get a larger jar to push yourself towards even bigger goals with more significant rewards like a weekend away with your sweetie or leasing a better vehicle.

4. Choose a buddy. Any day you DON'T hit your DIG, give them $5.

5. Streak. Record how many days in a row you can achieve your DIG. Set benchmarks (10, 20, 40, etc.) with increasing large rewards. Throw yourself a party when you reach 100!

Suppose you are like many professionals; just reading the ideas for DIG games got you a bit excited. Imagine that feeling 10x every day. Are your juices flowing? Are you excited by the challenge excited by the opportunity? Ready to rise and compete with yourself for greatness?

Welcome to Eustress. Enjoy the struggle!

In Chaos Hides Opportunity

Napoleon was marching, Europe in confusion. Markets were in free-fall, and uncertainty swept the land. Shops closed, businesses failed, and fear was in the streets. And Rothschild boldly made a fortune that would make Zuckerberg blush.

Plague gripped Europe. Entire towns were vacant, trade halted, universities shut down, and professors and students scattered. Sir Isaac Newton formulated his theory of gravity and wrote the basis of calculus.

Recession swept the United States. Oil embargoes strangled industry and daily life, and gas lines circled around the block. Economic prospects were dim, and wage controls suppressed hope for the future. Apple and Microsoft were born, spurring technology innovations and adoption and creating an untold number of millionaires.

Now is the time to be bold, to charge forward to glory. To build your empire.

Be not afraid, for cowards will never truly live.

Do not bunker and hunker down, expecting to outlast the storm because your defenses will collapse, and you will be a ruin. Ride out, face the fury, and earn your glory like Theoden King in JRR Tolkien's *The Lord of the Rings*.

Patience is a virtue, but fear is not. Pick up your phone, call your clients, and inspire them. Call those who did not become clients and offer to defend them. Acquire new clients by being bold and facing the demons of fear and panic. Inspire others, lead the charge, and beat back the chaos as you expand your kingdom.

Gird yourself for battle, for glory awaits as you protect those you serve from the terror sweeping the land. Ride out, boldly attack, and seize the field. Fight for your future and that of those you love.

Onward!

1 Percent

One out of one hundred white belts achieve the rank of black belt. Almost all start with the dream, but then reality hits, and they realize the work is needed, so they start dropping like flies.

One percent of internet community members contribute, and the other 99% lurk. They add nothing to the group.

The average American works 34 hours a week but is productive for only about 15. If you were productive for 7 hours a day, you would be in the top 1% of productive hours and probably also in the top 1% of income.

The top 1% of single-income earners in the US have a threshold of about $325k, and for married couples, it is $525k.

Be a 1% er.

Outwork others.

Out-think others.

Don't waste time like the others.

Then, eventually, you can do what 99% can't do because right now, you do what 99% can't or won't do as Grey stated in "The Common Denominator of Success" 90+ years ago.

Work like a 1% er, then live the life you want because by choosing to work hard and smart, you can choose whatever you want.

Trust The Process

"You have to fall in love with the process of becoming great."
Jeff Capel Everyone wants the glory.

The adulation.

The results.

Making a million dollars. Winning the title.

Getting that prize, be it the sexy sports car, gorgeous spouse, or dream house.

But you don't deserve it. Not until you've EARNED it.

Wealth, like power or fame, cannot be suddenly achieved without work without serious negative consequences.

"Strength does not come from winning. Your struggles develop your strengths."

Arnold Schwarzenegger You might get lucky and get that massive commission on a single sale, but if you haven't repeatedly failed and learned, then you didn't earn it. When that money is gone, it is gone because you didn't earn the scars and learn the lessons leading up to that big win that will guide you to winning again.

An early huge success is the worst thing that can happen to a rookie because it will poison your expectations and give you too much too quickly. Like the rock star with the monster hit, who didn't grind in the clubs and sleep in fleabag motels or the van as they cut their chops and built a following and skill set, they get the accolades, the groupies, and the fame, and then POOF, it disappears, never to return.

Easy come, easy go.

"Forces beyond your control can take away everything you possess except one thing: your freedom to choose how you will respond to the situation." Viktor Frankl in "Man's Search for Meaning".

Trust the process.

Know that your work may not show today but will in the weeks, months, and years to come.

Understand that today's practice produces tomorrow's champion.

"I make of myself a sacrifice unto myself," declared Odin as he suffered for wisdom. Sacrifice the enjoyment of today to your work to build a brighter future and a glorious career. Develop your plan and work it. Have faith in your activity and your vision.

Trust the process.

Follow the guidance of your mentors.

Follow your Standard Operating Procedures.

Practice daily to improve your skill set.

Feed your spirit daily to strengthen your mindset.

Make the little right choices throughout the day, the small sacrifices that lead to big victories later.

Toughen your resolve in the face of adversity.

Callous your mind as David Goggins says, so that the pains of failure along the way will not stop you from your ultimate goals. Love the daily practice to improve.

Hate losing enough to learn to win, to push through even when you are exhausted and feel you have nothing left to give.

Know that each of those steps brings you closer to the finish and that others won't reach it because they will quit while you never will.

Win each day, each hour. Fight to maximize each minute to be better tonight than you were when you awoke. Constantly strive for improvement. Trust the process.

And you will celebrate the success because you earned it.

One Bite

Sometimes, we have to trick ourselves, especially when we are tired or faced with something daunting, like staring up at the Cliffs of Insanity and saying, "I have to climb up there!?!"

So here are some tricks to help you get started, whether you're training for that 10km race, making the 50 dials you need to hit your goal, or running those introductory feeder lists for the week.

1. Lie to yourself but begin. "I'll only go around the block." Get ready, start with the idea of only doing the bare minimum. But once you get started you get rolling, and momentum is on your side instead of hampering you. One block becomes two, then four, and then you do your entire run. Having your phone list and making one dial turns into five, then fifteen, and then you look up and you are done.

2. Chunk the task. Set a timer on your phone for 18 minutes. Block out all the distractions and pound away at the phone, chipping away at the mountainous task with all you have for a slice of time. When the timer goes off, STOP. Get up and refill your coffee or walk around the building as a reward and reset your mind. Then sit down, reset the timer, and repeat until you have finished.

3. Bribe yourself. "When I run these lists, I can have a beer." I used this to reward/force myself to hit my weekly dialing goal as a new Rep for the first few years until I had the habit engraved in my soul.

4. Gamify it. Get a partner to compete against, place a bet (loser washes winner's car, a bottle of wine, loser wears a lime green leisure suit to the office, the winner gets the better parking spot, be creative!), and let the games begin. One thing: have an out. If you both hit your goal, you celebrate together.
5. Change of scenery. Have to make 25 dials today? Take your calendar, phone, and list, and sit in the closet until you're done. Next time, from your car. Or do it from someplace nice, like a cushy chair, so you'll want to stay after doing the first increment.

We all have things we don't want to do because they are so huge, or they are just stupid (think of all those CE classes...), or we are afraid of them. But you know the old saying of how you eat an elephant: one bite at a time. Get your fork, sharpen the knife, and pour some ketchup on that sucker and go.

Psychology and The IRS actually agree on something. The Internal Revenue Service has an ideal of "highest and best use" for an asset (say a chunk of land) that could be valued at what it is currently being utilized for (say, laying fallow, unused in a growing city, and almost worthless). Yet the IRS instead places the value for estate tax calculations based on its POTENTIAL, what that asset could reasonably be used for instead of what it is (developed in line with local regulations, usages, and values). And this is almost always a lot more than what the asset is currently doing.

You are that asset.

Dr. Jordan Peterson, best-selling author of "12 Rules for Life" and "Beyond Order," as well as a renowned clinical psychologist, asks, *"Who are you, and more importantly, who could you be if you were everything that you could conceivably be?"* Reflect on this for a moment.

None of us jumped out of the womb as fully formed individuals embodying our maximum potential, except Chuck Norris. The rest of us have had to determine what is important to us and invest time and money to try and clear the ground and build something of ourselves, be it a business or relationships or our physical health. We formed a vision of our potential, such as making the team in high school, playing that instrument in a concert, graduating college, building a family, our career, etc., and then had to do things to move it from fantasy to reality.

Some still dream and live in delusion and quietly despair, while others visualize and execute. The latter always struggle but can make progress towards their potential. It inevitably hurts, "but it's a good kind of hurt."

We shape our futures, and we do so by first forming a vision for what we would like that future to look like and then acting upon that. We flounder if we have a poor image of what we want (or worse yet, nothing to guide us). This is why many people are aimless in their lives and relationships, and careers and can end up in not good places: addictions, affairs, dead-end jobs, and friendships that suck their souls away. Those who take this road to nowhere ultimately have more pain (and create more for others) than those aiming at something better in their lives. *"A people without a vision will* perish," it says in the Book of Proverbs, and what applies to humanity as a whole applies equally to an individual human.

Those who at least know where the mountain is and start in that direction are better off than those sitting on the couch eating Cheetos and watching The Bachelor, even if their progress is slow. They stumble, sweat, and sometimes want to give up, but choosing to go higher is better. The views and experiences along the way, the process of becoming better, is worth the effort.

"Don't underestimate the power of vision and direction. These are irresistible forces that transform what might appear to be unconquerable obstacles into traversable pathways and expanding opportunities." Jordan B. Peterson points out in *12 Rules for Life.*

So, what is your vision?

What are you trying to build in your life?

Get off the couch and start moving in the direction of your dream. Start building that future because the tax bill for your psyche is coming due. It's better to create a prosperous life than watch others live theirs and have the massive cost of doubting what could have been.

Welcome Class

Settle down, please, class. I know everyone is excited and still probably mentally on summer vacation still, but it's time to buckle down and get to work.

First, my name is Mr. TIM, and I will be your instructor for this class. As background, I was like you two and a half decades ago, probably worse. Scrawny, lacking social skills, a total nerd. But my advantage over the other students was that I sought out people who knew more than I did and worked my butt off. Those of you who make that same sort of commitment will be between somewhat and wildly successful.

Secondly, there is the door for those who don't want to work. You might as well leave now so you don't waste your time and that of your peers. Seriously. If you are not willing to work to the point of exhaustion, don't bother. As my father taught me: *"Work half days. Any twelve hours will do."* You are not working at the DMV; you are compensated with results. If you are satisfied with being a sloth and sucking the oxygen from others, please exit stage right.

Third, this is not Shakespeare. This is business. If you mess up a single word of your script, the critics will not cry havoc and let the dogs of war loose on you. Communication is 90+ %, NOT the words you use, the carefully crafted rhetoric. It is your body language, confidence, belief in the words, and philosophies behind them. You will be powerful and persuasive if you have studied the logic and reason behind the words and believe their intent. Perfection is the enemy of The Great as surely as The Good is. Reflect on that.

That said, I expect and demand that you practice daily for at least an hour of hardcore, dedicated skill improvement. Within a day or two, I can tell which of you are exerting effort and which are destined to fail. I will not care about your future more than you do.

Fourth, while I expect you to pour your heart, soul, and brain into your development, I get that you aren't robots. You need to have outside interests to help you recharge, thus allowing you to bust your hump for those sixty hours a week you are working. I want you to do at least thirty minutes of physical activity daily, whatever form interests you. This is the minimal threshold for telomeric health, and a brain scan would indicate the increased mental acuity from a good half-hour of sweat. As Sir Richard Branson said, *"The greatest productivity tool is to work out more."*

I also want you to take the time to appreciate the beauty in the world around you because it is fleeting and will make your ultimate rewards sweeter, balancing effort and enjoyment. Watch the sunrise. Send pictures of flowers to those you love. Eat the chocolate. I might kick your butt, but this is not Sparta.

And finally, please remember this class: the most fantastic games are still just games. Business is a part of life; it is not the reason for life. Learning this is the ultimate path to sustainable success and happiness. Loving the effort to become a champion makes the results more likely; rest is as important as training. It is pushing hard but knowing when to lighten up. Humor is a counter to seriousness. This is the Yin and Yang of your future, and Jocko Willink summarizes it well in his book *The Dichotomy of Leadership*:

"So, what does it take to win? Yes, you have to be determined. Yes, you have to be driven. Yes, you must have the unconquerable will to win. But to really win, to truly win at all costs, requires more flexibility, more creativity, more adaptability, more compromise, and more humility than most people ever realize. That is what it takes to win."

Now, class, let's get to work.

Batman

Do you know why Batman is my favorite hero in the DC Comics universe?

Not because he fights with the Joker, my favorite bad guy (Don't try to psychoanalyze me. The Irish are immune to it, per Freud). It's because I could be Batman. So could you.

Hear me out.

Superman is an alien born with innate abilities powered by the sun. Being Irish, the sun isn't my friend; I must wear SPF5000 to open my sunroof. So, Superman-like abilities are a no-go.

Wonder Woman is the ultimate Amazon or a Goddess; we aren't sure which. But again, innate abilities beyond mere mortals.

Green Lantern? Aliens!

Martian Manhunter? Actual alien. Batman? Just a man.

An intelligent human who, through his will, training, and sacrifice, has made himself the most dangerous member of The Justice League.

Yeah, he has a utility belt and many toys he's built. But he knows how to use them. He practices.

Yeah, he has money. But he took what he had and made it orders of magnitude more. He thinks.

He has a strategy to take out every other member of the Justice League if they go rogue. He plans.

He's human.

He bleeds.

He sucks it up and keeps fighting.

He loses.

He recovers, figures out why, and fights again.

And Batman wins.

Because he refuses to stay down.

I could be Batman or at least have his mindset.

YOU can be Batman.

Study your opponents. Increase your knowledge.

Build your Will Set and Skill Set.

Don't rest on past victories.

Practice plan and execute.

Be Batman.

Scantiest

In 2023, I ran a Ragnar (a 200-ish team-mile relay race) for the first time in person in over two years. The night before, I slept outside on the ground in a sleeping bag, and it got cold and dewy. I was literally running on a few hours of sleep after a month of overextending myself personally and professionally and already being at my supposed human limits.

We were up by five and out the door by 5:30, and I would not get to lie down again until after 2:30 the following day.

How often do you push yourself to see what you are capable of? Ultrarunner (and former NAVY SEAL) David Goggins insists that every person has a governor in their mind that restricts their capabilities, set somewhere at 40% of their potential. This means you could quickly increase what you are doing by a quarter more than what you are doing and still only be at half capacity. What could you accomplish at work and personally? If you were that much better, could you go harder on that project or deeper into your relationships? You will surprise yourself with what you are capable of.

Most people are afraid to toughen their minds and bodies to become better. Generally People will avoid hard work if they can; the most demanding work is on us.

Especially in a world where we rarely lack material things, all of our physical needs are met now (especially in the way of shelter, safety, and, most of all, calories), and they are done so quickly that we are accustomed to comfort. This relative luxury inevitably harms us because the world is not all cupcakes and honeymoons; it is a place filled with pain, change, and inevitable challenges that we need to remember to prepare for.

Bad stuff is going to happen. The economy is going to go into the toilet every decade. Your family will change (as do the relationships within it), we all grow older, and sickness and death of those we care about are inevitable. We must remember that tough times are coming in all ways (as are more good times, as that is the world cycle). So, how do we appreciate the good we have but not become dependent upon it? How do we appreciate what we have but still survive without it?

"Set aside a certain number of days during which you shall be content with the cheapest fare, with coarse and rough dress, saying to yourself, "Is this the condition that I feared?" Seneca.

Various religions fast for a period, and when the fast is broken, all food is better than it would be. If you have had mouth surgery and been unable to eat for a week, you know exactly what I mean.

Separation from the norm allows us to appreciate the everyday things we take for granted, like going out to see people post-COVID or sending the kids to school and getting a break. Even the little things like a good morning from your sweetie are craved if it is no longer there, so when it does return (if you are lucky that way), the moment is that much sweeter because of the hiatus and being able to know what it would be like to lack that completely. We survive, but if the joyful person/thing returns, we treasure the moments as precious because we know the loss thereof. Every kiss becomes as precious as the first.

You have a chance today to push your limits and remove your governor. You also have the opportunity to choose minor hardships to welcome the more accessible patches and moments of beauty via contrast.

I run in the rain because I hate it. But it makes me appreciate the shower and dry clothes after. And the next dry run is that much more enjoyable because of the contrast. When I had to run in a monsoon during a race, it wasn't that much of a stretch because I chose to know how soggy wet socks feel. I have calloused my mind, as Goggins would say. Seneca would approve.

So, when we finally got to the sleeping place at early o'clock, the only spot available was on gravel. It didn't matter; I laid out my bag, curled up, and was out in a few minutes until someone's car alarm went off at 4:00.

I could roll back over and get another half hour of sleep after that. But the two-ish hours of sleep after crazy hard runs and sleep deprivation were like Morpheus had chosen me because I was completely invigorated—or at least convinced me of that—and ran well. I rocked the hardest, longest leg of the race. I knew I could because I was mentally tough from pushing myself and forcing myself to be uncomfortable when I didn't have to.

That night after the race, I slept on a couch outside, and those five hours were terrific!

Those who have battled for what they have appreciate it more than those who have had it handed to them. The earned beer is the best one. The difficult victory is the sweetest, and returning to the harsh conditions that made you a champion, even when you don't have to, can keep you on top.

Choose the hard path; otherwise, life will force you onto it, and you won't be prepared for it.

"Every difficulty in life gives us an opportunity to turn inward and invoke our inner resources. The trials we endure can and should introduce us to our strengths. Prudent people look beyond the incident and seek to form the habit of putting it to good use. On the occasion of an accidental event, don't just react haphazardly: remember to turn inward and ask what resources you have for dealing with it. Dig deeply. You possess strengths you might not realize you have. Find the right one. Use it." Epictetus Develop those resources. Test yourself with trials and tribulations when you don't have to, to temper your spirit as steel is tempered in the flame.

"Fire is the test of gold; adversity of strong men." Seneca Test yourself when you don't have to so that you can pass the tests of life when you do have to. You will find you have resources you didn't realize and strengths you were unaware of.

Maybe you'll even run a Ragnar. On too little sleep, because with adversity, you will find that you have just enough to succeed.

Thankful

We are approaching Thanksgiving, and showing gratitude has been directly linked to increased happiness and productivity.

So be thankful that you opted for a sales career in financial services. Here are five reasons why you should be grateful:

1. You can sell more if you want to make more money. While your friends in corporate America must wait until their next salary action or work more hours to make more money, you can just go sell more.
2. Speaking of selling more. Almost everyone wants and needs what you have for them:

    a. About 40% of Americans say they want more life insurance.

    b. The vast majority of Americans own NO individual Disability Insurance.

    c. The majority of Millennials say they want a guaranteed income in retirement.

    d. Gen Z wants to save at a higher rate than any previous generation.

    e. Most Baby Boomers will need Long Term Care, and Long-Term Care Insurance is the most effective way to meet their demands.

    f. Tax rates are going to go up, making tax-favored savings/investments (annuities and life insurance and 529 Plans) that are much more attractive.

3. Whenever there is uncertainty (in the markets, with tax policy, with the general economy or job market, etc.) people seek professional guidance.
4. Speaking of uncertainty, we have seen a massive shift in the employment landscape. Something like 20% of Americans lost their jobs during the COVID-19 pandemic, a significant number of people retired, and the talent competition is so fierce that people across all economic strata are being wooed by competitors and getting big raises for switching companies. I think you can see several opportunities in this.
5. The entire market has embraced remote meetings. You can now move electrons instead of molecules. No more finding a parking spot and paying for it, wasting 20-30 minutes per meeting minimum traveling. You can work shorter hours, see more clients, and increase revenue.

Take a few minutes to think about these opportunities and write down how you can use the information presented above to increase your revenue significantly.

Then, be thankful and share your gratitude and happiness with others.

The Struggle is Real

Everyone wants it easy—easy sales, easy relationships, green lights from the garage to the office, and coffee waiting with zero problems at work—maybe a nice chair massage, a bonus, and a cupcake with butterflies floating around.

That's a fantasy, and if you are going to fantasize, it should at least have the potential to occur, like going to Tahiti with the love of your life once the chaos subsides.

"The bravest sight in the world is to see a great man struggling with adversity." Seneca proclaimed millennia ago. Not Sisyphus eternally pushing his rock up the hill only to have it crash back down repeatedly, but to watch a flawed human exerting themselves in a worthy cause or someone exhibiting excellence and ignoring limits.

As an athlete, I find the Olympics entertaining and inspiring. But the Paralympics inspire me to overcome obstacles on an entirely new level. Whatever doubts I have, I watch videos of athletes like these and tell myself, "Your excuse is invalid."

I have seen people overcome issues and fight for their beliefs and goals in ways that put me to shame, be it John Nichols (from a broken neck to running marathons and leading NAIFA), my autistic son completing Cub Scouts, or that single mom working two jobs and trying to go to school to build a better life for herself and her kids. It isn't easy, but it's worth it.

"Nothing in the world is worth having or worth doing unless it means effort, pain, difficulty...I have never envied a human

being who led an easy life." President Theodore Roosevelt was a Nobel Peace Prize Winner, Congressional Medal of Honor Recipient, a bestselling author, and a severe asthmatic as a child. His early struggles with health, the loss of his parents, and the death of his wife could have broken him but didn't, making him the leader he became for the rest of his life.

The cecropia moth is massive and beautiful, with its six-inch wingspan. It also has an incredibly thick cocoon it has to break out of after its metamorphosis. Struggling against what had held it in and protected it strengthens the moth's wings so that it can fly. Making it easy by cracking the cocoon steals the opportunity to overcome adversity from the moth, and it never becomes strong enough to fly. To fly, one must not give up.

The snowplow parents who clear the way for their kids? It becomes too easy, and they never develop their strength and resiliency and are stunted in their growth. It's better to make it more rigid (not 1970s latchkey kid level, but definitely not pampered) so that they become better.

Muscles only grow because they overcome resistance.

The most difficult victories are the sweetest, as are the rewards afterward for the greatest of struggles.

Do not wish for lighter burdens but for a stronger back. For the will to work to develop yourself and not to give in. Strengthen yourself, build your guts and faith like you would a muscle, and be better able to get the job done instead of wishing it were easy or avoiding the tough work altogether.

Hannibal and The Way

I have a friend, "Tommy the Firefighter". We have been friends since we were eighteen and have seen each other grow into leaders. A few years back, Tommy and I talked about problem-solving, and he told me about a conversation with one of his early trainers at the firehouse.

Trainer: So, there is a fire in the house. How do you get in?

Tommy: Through the door.

Trainer: The door is on fire. Tommy: Through the window. Trainer: It's got bars over it.

Tommy Through the wall. Trainer: Why?

Tommy: There are people in there to save. I have to get in there somehow.

Think about this conversation that impacted an 18-year-old kid who carries a core belief three decades later and is employed to overcome professional losses and health issues.

Have to get in there; flame and fixtures be damned.

There are people to save, even if it is yourself.

Don't get stuck or fixated on what has happened or the barriers before you. Go over them, around them, or through them.

Slice the Gordian Knot and solve the unsolvable with different thinking.

Did COVID-19 change how you interact with clients? Adapt yourself to the situation. Can't shake hands or touch them on the shoulder to establish rapport? How about a micro-video to convey your personality? Share a meme about homeschooling while working. Use a caricature for your avatar or change your Zoom background to reflect who you are so your clients can get your vibe and connect with you.

Get in there to save the people.

As Hannibal proclaimed, *I will find a way or make a way.*

Make your way into where you need to be.

Have trouble getting that potential client to pick up the phone? Have your client send a mutual introduction text to the two of you and hand you off to that person with their full imprimatur.

"What stands in the way becomes the way." Marcus Aurelius.

"Innovation is not born from the dream; innovation is born from the struggle." <u>Simon Sinek</u>.

"Good leaders don't make excuses. Instead, they figure out a way to get things done." Jocko Willink Lead. Adapt and overcome.

Get in there; there are people to save.

Path of Most Resistance

I was listening to a podcast while working out the other morning, and a single line from it resonated with me and echoed something in my soul, making me stop mid-pushup and rush over to the computer to capture the concept. Restated in a slightly more poetic way, the idea is:

The path of most resistance is the way to excellence.

In the intro to "Courage is Calling," Stoic author Ryan Holiday retells one of my favorite Greek myths about Hercules. Even though his father was Zeus and he exhibited great strength and fighting ability, Hercules was just another demigod early in his life until he came to a crossroads. On each fork stood a goddess, offering him something and trying to woo him to her ways. One presented an easy life, great fame, earthly power, and riches. A life of luxury, but he would grow old as a mortal (even the greatest succumb to age and death) amid his comforts and pleasures, and eventually pass to Elysium but in a few generations be essentially forgotten other than some statues.

The other goddess offered pain, sacrifice, suffering, loneliness, grief, and doubt. But she also held potential: immortality if he could grasp it. His name will be remembered for as long as heroes are discussed, and he will have a place among the undying on Olympus if he accepts the risks and conquers the challenges. Hercules chooses the latter path, the rough road filled with danger, and he sits among the gods for it.

Robert Frost told a similar tale:

> *Two roads diverged in the wood, and I-*
>
> *I took the one less traveled by*
>
> *And that has made all the difference.*

The lane that others have not trod is more difficult but yields greater rewards, better views, and stories others wish they could tell because that dangerous path leads to adventures.

Take the rocky road. Accept the challenges. The scars you receive on your journey of the hero will be mementos of lessons and victories.

Accessible routes lead to a complicated and forgettable life. The un-blazed trail leads to glory and a story that will be remembered.

Choose the more brutal way because, in the end, you and the world will be better for it.

Pain

"You gain knowledge through suffering." David Goggins.

Pain is a crucible that reveals our impurities and allows us to separate the dross from the superior metal. Adversity, be it mental, emotional, or physical, will enable us to grow and become better versions of ourselves than before the trials and tribulations.

The worst agonies are those that are unexpected and that we are completely unprepared for. The car accident killed a close friend. The love of your life is leaving. The company you have sacrificed for a decade terminating your division out of the blue. The cancer diagnosis. All of us will be blindsided in a massive way at some point.

There is little we can do to prepare for these individual, specific events. Still, we can make ourselves stronger and better overall by *"callous your mind,"* as Goggins proclaims, so that when the truly horrible happens, we can be as prepared as possible. Or, as psychologist Jordan Peterson says: *"You aren't a sniveling worthless mess but can be useful in tragedy and strong for others."* But how?

The Stoics talked of choosing adversity. Of occasionally dressing in *"the meanest of clothes"* and *"partaking in the worst of fares"* so that poverty and loss do not frighten you as you are hardened to them. Catholics and Muslims fast for this reason, and that first bite afterward is the most delicious thing you can think of. Stoics further remind us to memento mori: remember death and face our mortality and that of those we care for so that we enjoy their presence more while we have them and are prepared for their loss and the void in our life their absence will cause. Appreciating the fragility of good fortune and life itself will help us get off the hedonic treadmill, as Lori Santos points out in the Yale course "Science of Well-Being" (available for free on <u>Coursera</u>). Build resilience for the inevitable massive shock of loss.

Choose to take the difficult path once in a while. Take an ice-cold shower. Run in the blistering heat or freezing rain. Go on a spartan diet for a few days. Put yourself in mental duress and challenge your assumptions. Push your limits. The more often you choose to make yourself uncomfortable, the more comfortable you will become going through the inevitable rough patches. The contrast between the hardships you decided to endure versus your normal comfortable existence will prepare you for the inevitable pain that is part of life. The greater the disparity you force yourself into, the stronger your foundation to withstand the assault that will break lesser people.

If you select the easy path, life will ultimately be hard and potentially break you. But if you choose to hurt yourself over and over by taking the hard route, ultimately, your life will be easier. You decide when and how much you want to suffer. What will you opt for?

Love It

"I Love It!"

How often do you say that when faced with adversity? Why not?

Why do you want it easy?

"The obstacle is the way," proclaims the Stoics, and it is true.

"Easy come, easy go" describes money, power, fame, and clients. Those who jump in bed with you easily jump out as quickly, as fickle as Lady Luck.

But what takes work and you must struggle to acquire cannot be taken away. "I wear my black belt on my soul, not my waist," one champion declared.

You were not meant to have success without work because you won't appreciate it nor be able to replicate it. It's like hitting the lottery for a quarter million dollars. Quick hit, but what will you do when it's gone?

"The only way to do great work is to love what you do." Steve Jobs

"Nothing in the world is worth having or worth doing unless it means effort, pain, difficulty...."

Teddy Roosevelt That hard thing? Attempt it.

The thing that scares you? Do it.

Make that call.

Ask for that Introduction.

Fight for what you want, be it success or love.

Want it bad enough to taste it, bad enough to sacrifice for it?

Desire success and greatness more than comfort and the cocoon you inhabit.

Birds fly because of the pressure on their wings.

Diamonds are formed in heat and pressure. Muscles grow through resistance.

Champions want a challenge.

The easy road leads to Hell, the hard way to Heaven.

Embrace the daily struggle, the wrestling with adversity, the crucible that fires your steel.

Love your battle, and you will be victorious.

Not Giving a F*ck

"The Subtle Art of Not Giving a F*CK" by Mark Manson embodies Stoicism for the 2020s, with more F-bombs than Marcus Aurelius used, because 2020 to today deserves all the F-bombs in the arsenal.

By not caring too much, you can work towards something but not be so focused that when the Universe decides to take it to the next level and release the chain-saw-wielding mutated economists or whatever the hell is coming next month, you can just roll with the punches and move on.

Alan Watts calls it "The Backwards Law": *the more you want something, the more you work for something, the less likely you are to get it.*

Because if you care too much about it, you're trying too hard. It interferes with your Flow. Care, but just enough, and only as long as is appropriate. That is the secret to success.

The Tao Te Ching talks about doing your job, putting down your tools, and returning to your life—be it the weapons of war or your computer. Do the job, care enough to do it well, and move on without the emotional baggage.

Two monks were walking in a rainstorm, and a young woman was stuck on a rock and in danger. The older monk picked her up, carried her to safety, and moved on. An hour later, the younger monk, still upset at violating their oath not to touch a female, berated the helping monk. The older and wiser monk, NGAF (Not Giving a F*CK), replied, "I put the woman down on the river edge. How long will you carry her?"

SMACK! Shut it, whelp!

Carrying guilt for doing what had to be done in a time of chaos to save another is giving a F*CK that you should save for something more important. And being upset over someone else doing this is not your responsibility, so keep your nose in your own business, Karen. No, you CAN'T talk to the manager!

F*CKs are a limited resource. We only have so many to give. So, what are you giving them to?

That idiot that cuts you off on the way to the office, that you road rage against and let take one of your valuable F*CKs for the day? Just say "F-you" mentally and forget them, move on, and actually save that F*CK for something important.

Does a potential client say, "No, I don't want your service that will make my life better, save me money, and outsource the caring about this issue to you, the professional, instead of me half-assing it myself"? Don't waste additional F*CKs beyond what you already have. Just move on. Save that F*CK to try and help someone else, someone who does give an F.

Are kids only going to school a quarter of the time this fall? Oh well. Instead of railing against the Governor or the idiots not following/believing basic science or getting into a flaming debate On Facebook, just say, "Oh well," move forward, and figure out how to deal with it. As my mom (an educator) always said, never let school interfere with your education. Give a F*CK about creating a desire for knowledge instead of checking boxes; it's more important overall.

Only care about the important things. If it's not important, it isn't worth wasting one of your valuable F's on.

Oh, they only have 85% lean beef instead of 93%. No F given; roll with it. Pour off the extra fat and suck it up.

Did the client have to reschedule because of an issue with the kid? If you have five clients scheduled daily, one needing to meet next week instead of today shouldn't financially impact you if you run a high-activity business. So don't waste an F; just re-allocate the time to other business activities.

Spill coffee all over your shirt? Bitch for 30 seconds and move on. Also, keep an extra shirt in your office because EVERYONE spills coffee all over the place at one point or another. Don't waste an F, and plan to minimize the inevitable disaster.

Lose a case? Find another.

Lose out in competition? Get better. Win next time and more often in the future. Invest your F in maximizing your abilities, not in that one where you weren't the best. Care about becoming the best; you won't care about losing as much.

Did your car engine blow up on the highway on the way to the office? Move it to a phone conference and do it while waiting for the tow truck. Give an F about getting a new car so you can get back to mobile and make money with more incentive to succeed. Focus on the big goal, not the little things in the way of the goal. I did.

I care about the big things, not the little time or energy-wasting things. That's why Steve Jobs wore the same outfit type: so he could grab and go and not care about it. That's why, for 15+ years, I only had white dress shirts: so I could avoid using an F on whether my lavender shirt matched my violet tie. F it, white shirt, blue suit, almost any tie in the closet, and GO!

According to Proverbs 29:18, "A people without a vision perish." If they really care about nothing, everything is the end of the world, and they expend their energy on minuscule issues, disperse their strength, and expire.

John F Kennedy Jr. cared about getting The US to the Moon. He didn't give a hoot about the new technologies we had to build, the cost, or the fact that the Russians were ahead of us in the Space Race. He had a BHAG (Big Hairy Audacious Goal) that the country bought into, to put a man on the Moon by the end of the decade. And JFK didn't live to see it happen, but the country still gave the F to get us there. Because we had saved up the will and reserves and didn't waste them on trivial crap. Not giving an F about stupid stuff gives you the power to focus and achieve meaningful things.

So, guard your reserves, given the chaos and confusion of this decade, that will only get worse from the sounds of it. Focus on the big things in your life, not the inevitable little bumps on the road to the mountain of success. Don't give a F*CK until it is time to really give one, and then do so because it really matters. That is how we will make it through to next year and succeed in this one.

Not My Circus

There is an old Polish saying: *not my circus, not my monkeys.*

Some things are not our problem—most things, actually.

The Stoics teach us to control what we can (our effort, attitude, thoughts, and reactions to external events). We can't control the weather (but we can learn and create contingencies like having rain gear and backup plans); we can't control the Administration and what they legislate (although we can influence it through organizations like <u>NAIFA</u> that collect our voices and amplify them); we can't control whether someone else is having a bad day before we talk to them. We can just do our best in the situation to understand, act with empathy where we can, and improve things as we advance within the constraints given and our spheres of control/influence.

And sometimes, we just need to walk away.

Now, if the monkeys are yours because it is your circus (probably the best description of home life these days), then you have to deal with the issues before they spiral out of control, and you have a Lord of The Flies situation. But if it is someone else's circus, and they haven't invited you into their big top (whether as a performer, or guest, or maybe to help be ringmaster), then just let it be.

"Poor planning on your part does not constitute an emergency on mine" was something I heard as an 18-year-old Pledge in the Fraternity, a nicer (or more management speak) way of saying "you made your bed, you lie in it" as my mother would tell her brood. We can't solve everyone else's problems, nor should we. Pay attention to yourself, Karen (or Chad), because the manager isn't going to talk to you!

We want to save others, put on our super suit, rescue the kittens in our White Knight armor, and save the damsel in distress. News flash: many people are happy in their misery, or at least claim to be because they are unwilling to do what it takes to correct their situation, be it breaking an addiction or having the discipline to eat right and exercise or do the extra work to change their economic conditions. Some will never change because their situation isn't painful enough for them to force their metamorphosis. It can rip your soul to shreds watching a friend deteriorate or, to a lesser level, watching clients make completely irrational and self-destructive decisions. Sometimes we need to let them fail, to hit rock bottom before we help them climb out of the pit of despair. Getting to the bottom is where a foundation for growth is built.

A drowning person is dangerous to save because they will unconsciously fight and flail and drag you under with them. Lifeguards know they need to push this person away so that they don't go under; when the person in need of rescue is exhausted and has expended everything, they can be dragged out of danger and truly helped on stable land. Think about that and how you might talk to them while staying out of harm's way.

As a profession, we help people in general and our clients in precise ways. It gives us skill sets and mindsets used in volunteer organizations and interpersonal relationships to improve operations, outlooks, and outcomes. Yet sometimes, others just can't see what we see because they look out for experiences we can't understand. You can care for them more than anyone who hasn't shared their last name (and sometimes even more), but until they open their tent and invite us into the inner workings of the circus, we can't let their monkeys get on our backs.

Marathon

If you want to run a marathon, you don't just get off the couch, throw on some sneakers and go.

You set the goal, put together a training plan, and start ramping up the miles over an extended training period.

You have to make sacrifices: go to bed early to rest and recover and get up for those early miles over long distances. You alter your diet, you listen to inspirational stories and put together playlists to motivate you when it is cold and wet out and you just don't feel like doing it.

But you do it.

Or else you won't hit that Big Goal.

Why aren't you doing the same with your business?

Running a marathon is awesome; I've done it a couple dozen times. But having a full schedule all the time of great clients and working 10-hour days every day actually doing the fun client-facing stuff like asking questions and telling stories and filling out lots of paperwork because of the consistent stream of business from high-quality introductions is not shabby, especially when you have the cash flow to do whatever you want when not working, such as flying to someplace sunny and beautiful to do a marathon.

Approach your business like a marathon.

Get enough rest and get up early. Make yourself go a little harder and farther each week and build in recovery times.

Read what others have done. Get friends that you can train with who can support and push each other and hold you accountable. Write out your goals, work on your technique, and do what you need to every day starting now so that six months from now, you can go the distance you want.

Do it.

If you never challenge yourself, you'll regret it at some point. "I could have" is the absolute worst thing to say if you never really tried. Doubts linger, but the experience of doing something exceptional will live in you forever.

Get off the couch.

Get your plan together. Get moving.

3 Rules

I did my first race when I was 29, and as with all intense endurance endeavors, there are lessons to be learned from it. Essentially, there are three rules for multistage events (triathlons, Ragnars, business, and life) that should allow you to finish strong if you have done your prep work.

Leg One: Don't be an Idiot.

Leg Two: Don't be a Hero.

Leg Three: Don't be a Wimp.

It's that simple, but it's sure not easy. Running thirty miles in a day is simple (just put one foot in front of the other, over and over), but it's not easy, either. Building a business (picking up the phone and calling people repeatedly) or living (getting up and doing your best over and over) is also not easy.

Don't be an Idiot. We all want to come out of the gate hot because we are so excited. We've been prepping for this and want to get at it hard and quickly. It doesn't matter if it is the swim in the triathlon or that first day in a new position: we are a little anxious, a little overzealous, and probably overconfident. The best thing to do is observe others who have been there and done that. Observe, ask questions, listen. Heed the warnings of the race directors (or management or spiritual leaders, as the case may be). Start hard but not too hard because you must keep the pace up. Find someone to track and stay with for a bit that seems to be slightly better than yourself. You might have to drop off a little, or as you get deeper, you can be better, so focus on someone new to benchmark yourself against. Don't be an Idiot; stay within yourself and learn every step of the way in this part to set the expectation for the other two stages.

Don't be a Hero. We tend to go beyond our abilities once we get through the first leg and have a good handle on our feelings. On the race course, we want to drop the hammer and overtake all the other competitors; we try to do the same thing at work. But we have already used a lot of physical and emotional energy and tried to do things we shouldn't. We probably are low on sleep and running on caffeine. We take on clients way beyond our capability (because we've been told to fake it until we make it), or arrogance creeps in, and we get off our game plan and go way too hard to try and win the race in the still too early stages. We take unnecessary risks. We don't rely on our team for the support we should (ego is the enemy, as Ryan Holiday reminded us of, and the course will, too) and think we can do it on our own. This is the most dangerous stage, be it the bike in the triathlon, the second leg of the Ragnar, or your time a little past being a rookie where others start to look up to you in the office. This is where we need to do it right and be able to have the guts to say "no". No, I'm not going to cut corners, burn bridges, or sacrifice myself to try and get that little bit extra, be it sales or seconds. Don't be a Hero because you will flame out and become a warning to others.

Don't be a Wimp. Ok, last stage. You got this. This is where you are running off of experience and muscle memory and your vision of finishing, tapping into that feeling to overcome the exhaustion of getting to this point in the race. This is where it literally is the marathon (triathlon) or the bulk of your earnings (career). This is the point where you know you need your support crew and have no shame in tapping into them, taking a pause to get nourishment, to having someone tell you, "You can do it! Finish strong!". It is going to hurt. That's the fact of life and dealing with the pain of all the buildup of lactic acid and fatigue and everything else is the most important skill, just like navigating the political environment and little trip-ups at work is what stands between you and victory. This is where you have difficult conversations with clients and yourself, and if you wimp out, you won't win what you want. This is where you tap into the emotional strength from all that training and belief in yourself and your goal. Suck it up and empty your tank; you can rest afterward!

Everything is a race, something you have been prepping for with everything that has come before. The Three Rules (Don't be an Idiot, Don't Be a Hero, Don't Be a Wimp) need to guide each leg or else you won't finish how you could or should.

Championship Blues

Ever hit that big goal and then have nothing left emotionally for a while? A post-partum feeling of emptiness and maybe even depression, the blues and blahs after hitting MDRT, having your best year ever, or running that marathon?

Yeah, me too.

The greater the accomplishment, the greater the valley after climbing the mountain of achievement. After doing my double marathon, it hit me harder than Mike Tyson teeing off on an obnoxious clown.

I had a mentor, one of the top producers in the HISTORY of his company (one of the big three in the industry), who every January was clinically depressed as he stacked great production up year after year. Many a champion gets into a funk after taking the title. Climbing the mountain is more exciting and invigorating than the hike down.

So how do we make sure that success does not turn into suck?

Know that it is coming. Acknowledge the potential of the downturn emotionally after success.

Schedule some self-time. It's smart to pamper yourself after a race or celebrate hitting that goal.

Take time off. The day after a Ragnar or other huge physical activity, I will take a few walks to stretch my legs, but I won't actually run for three or four days. A couple of days after the end of a work deadline, I schedule off and disappear and unplug. When I finish writing a book, I don't look at it for a few days.

Come back with a plan. I ease back into running with an easy run, then a little longer a few days later, and then a longer one with cross-training scheduled. For work, I go non-client-facing for a day, half my normal load, then full load within a few days, then up to overload for maybe a week to get in the swing of things after a week and jump on the new period's goals.

Talk to someone. Maybe not a professional, but for a few days after an event, my running team checks in with each other to make sure no one slips too low. The same goes for my study group.

Challenging ourselves is part of human nature and is what allows us to achieve success personally and professionally. But rest and recovery are equally important, whether mentally or for muscles. Knowing that we will be sore and tired after we push our limits is part of the self-knowledge required for growth, and getting through the rough patches is part of the training of life.

Will And Work

Want to win? All it takes is the Two W's. Will. Work.

Will and Work. That's it.

Will is developed over the years by pushing yourself in uncomfortable ways, choosing the less easy path that develops your internal reserves of strength, having slightly uncomfortable discussions until they are no longer uncomfortable, and then being prepared to go to the edge of that new comfort zone again and again to expand your horizons.

By running further on the treadmill today than last week, which is further than the week before or the week before. Pushing your physical limit so that you have greater endurance and know the difference between tired and completely spent will push through the first by letting your Will command your body instead of vice versa.

Skipping some meals so that you know the feeling of hunger again can help you overcome those pangs and not let them distract you.

Cold showers or running in the rain on purpose, even though you hate it. By choosing a difficult, uncomfortable situation, you develop the mental muscles of discipline that can be used to overcome any burden in life because your Will becomes indomitable and stronger than the barriers in your way.

Will power is the greatest power a human can develop.

And then Work.

Do the work.

Grind it out.

Do the little things that lay the groundwork for the big stuff.

Do the steps. A marathon is 26.2 miles for everyone. There is no shortcut.

Work.

Pick up the phone and call the clients. Run the analysis and variations thereof. Ask ALL the hard questions (of everyone, including yourself), and your Will allows you to face them without flinching.

Put in the needed hours; even when exhausted, tap into those reserves built on the treadmill and work the long days and nights required to bring your dream from fantasy to reality.

Work.

Work and love every moment, knowing that it is for your purpose, that you are getting closer to your goal, and that nothing will stop you because of your Will that powers the Work.

W and W.

That is the only secret to success.

Vent

OK, I am going to vent.

And if you have delicate sensibilities, skip to the last line.

What the hell are you doing?

Why aren't you working?

You control your entire destiny; instead, you are fooling around and not working.

I provide you with motivational and educational pieces to fire you up and give you all the skills needed to build a highly profitable Introduction-Based Business.

Instead of following my guidance, you struggle and bitch and moan about not having any money.

I gave you the freaking treasure map! And the shovels. Get off yer ass and dig for that booty! Arggghh, Matey!

"Oh, it's SOOO tough calling people." Yeah, it is. Yet every experienced producer in your office?

They did it. I do it. **I HATE picking up the phone**, yet I do it. Why can't you? Are you scared that they are going to reach through the phone and death touch you? Leave a bad Yelp review? Call your mommy and say mean things about you?! Suck it up and dial or pack up and leave now because you are sucking the oxygen out of the office and wasting your manager's time.

"There is so much paperwork!" Too bad. There is as much paperwork applying for unemployment insurance. And paperwork means you get paid. Think of it as a time tax, the side effect of producing and making money.

"But..." No buts. Get off yours. Get to work.

Look, I have given you all the tools—the verbiage, the mental training, the answers to objections, the agendas, feeder lists, introduction Questions, and everything else I have used to succeed.

Everything but ME.

Do you know why you're a loser and I'm not? Because I hate losing enough to do the work to win. I get out of bed when tired and get going. I faced the things I was afraid of, and even if I hated them, I still did them each day, so I got what I wanted. I am working after 10:00 p.m. You're not. That is the difference.

I want it. You say you want it. I work to get it. You don't. It's that simple.

I work. You whine. Case closed.

Pick up the tools I gave you and get to work.

Do Not Go Quietly

"Focus and finish." My eight-year-old son with ADHD has heard these words in his Tae Kwon Do class numerous times.

"Champions run through the finish line."

"I didn't hear no bell." Rocky, to Tommy Gunn.

"I don't stop when I'm tired; I stop when I'm done." David Goggins I just ran my tenth Ragnar, a 200-ish-mile team relay race where each runner usually does three legs for somewhere between 15 and 20 miles. 18.3 for me this time.

With cracked ribs.

And a bruised sternum.

It was, at times, agony. But I didn't give up because others were depending on me to finish my job.

Do you stop when you are tired or when you are finished?

As a kid on the farm, we didn't stop until the harvest was in because once the rain came, we couldn't continue. Taught me to finish the job.

Dr. Stolk almost cut his hand off with a chainsaw but was back the next day, bucking up a tree. Why? "Job wasn't done."

Have you finished the job?

How often do you see other people in your office fail to succeed because they quit just before achieving their goals?

Why run a marathon to give up before the last .2 miles after doing the first 26?!

Are you digging and stopping three feet from gold?

Make that extra call.

Ask that one last client.

Give your all for one more day, one more week.

"Winning means you are willing to go longer, work harder, and give more than anyone else."

Vince Lombardi

"In life, you have three choices: give in, give up, or give it your all." Charleston Parker.

Your momma didn't raise a quitter. My mother taught me "suck it up" at an early age. Quit your bitching, take a slug of coffee and a deep breath, and tackle this thing.

Because you got this.

Will Power

Why did Tiger Woods dominate golf for a decade?

How did Senator John McCain and others survive the Hanoi Hilton as Prisoners of War in Vietnam?

How did a pudgy guy with social anxiety and a lisp become the greatest insurance salesman the world has ever known? Ben Feldman sold more life insurance than 90% of the companies in the US, yet he had to stand behind a screen to speak at MDRT because he was so scared of embarrassing himself.

How did people such as Viktor Frankl survive the horrors of the Nazi Concentration camps?

These people shared one characteristic that gave them the edge: indomitable willpower. The Stoics, such as Marcus Aurelius, believed that *"You have power over your mind, not outside events. Realize this, and you will find strength."*

This internal power gave Frankl freedom in the most horrible circumstances and gave McCain, Stockdale, and others the strength to endure.

"Successful people do what unsuccessful people can't or won't." Albert Grey proclaimed to NALU (now NAIFA) in 1940

Resolve or will is the mental muscle of success.

It must be strengthened through resistance.

Resisting the urge to give up and stop before the mission is accomplished, resisting fatigue, resisting the lure of average and mediocrity.

Resistance to the snooze button or the guarantees that sacrifice dreams instead of sacrificing FOR your dreams.

Resistance to taking the easy route instead of saying to yourself, "alpha up," and having a difficult conversation with yourself and your client.

Being a champion is not a choice but a thousand micro decisions every single day for years on end, each one bending the curve of the future towards a more desirable outcome by resisting giving in to the moment for a better future. Each choice is a micro-step towards greatness because of the will needed to take that one step.

You probably aren't blessed with superhuman hand-eye coordination, but you can choose to practice more, even after those with natural talents have quit.

You might not be 6'6" with the metabolism of a teenager. But you can decide not to eat the tasty cupcake and instead make a healthier choice.

You don't have movie star good looks but can get up and do the workout.

You can practice your language daily and remind yourself by writing ten times a day, "I deserve 10 introductions today," to build your will set so that when faced with a client that offers resistance, you can overcome it because your belief system is stronger than theirs. Because you have mental toughness from training yourself that they can't comprehend.

In our world, your skill set is not as important as your will to determine the outcome.

Set your will, and you will set your destiny for success.

From Frankl to Tiger to Feldman, the will to win transcends the game they play to unleash the indomitable spirit they developed through adversity.

Do Not Go Gently

Do not go gentle into that goodnight,

Old age should burn and rave at close of day.

Rage, rage against the dying of the light.

- <u>Dylan Thomas</u>

Do you burn?

Do you rave and rage?

Do you go gently home at the end of the day, or do you fight until the last minute, expending your strength on the field every day and leaving empty?

Are you mentally drained by the end of your day because you have been going since early o'clock and gave it your full effort repeatedly, through failure and triumph and failure again?

"Failure will never overtake me if my determination to succeed is strong enough." Og Mandino

"The vision of a champion is bent over, drenched in sweat, at the point of exhaustion, when nobody else is looking." <u>Mia Hamm</u> If you lose the morning, do you battle until you have won the day before retiring to rest?

Rage, rage against the dying of the light.

"Give up, give in, or give it your all." Charleston Parker Burn your ships each morning, so you can only go home victorious. Unleash your passion.

Attack each task with ferocious pride and a burning desire to win. Pour your soul into your work, from inception to completion.

Do not go gentle into that goodnight.

90 Percent

Everyone looks at me and assumes I am this perfectly tuned, disciplined machine because I run marathons, win martial arts championships, run a high-activity practice, and write daily. I've got it all figured out and can balance kids, health, work, charity, and relationships, not realizing that I am on a unicycle that's on fire while juggling chainsaws and trying to avoid the potholes filled with dynamite.

Every day is chaos; I have become comfortable managing it and ensuring that the important things get done and the whole shebang doesn't explode. Most days, it doesn't.

I use my SAM Suite® to manage my sales activities and my CRM to keep track of notes and set reminders. I use the Pomodoro method in writing (setting a timer for 18-22 minutes of focused effort) and have learned to say "No" to many things because the good is the enemy of the great.

I read, work out as soon as I get up to get it done and try to eat early at the office daily. For those that don't know, that means doing what I hate (for me it is phoning) to get it done and over with early while I still have willpower. You have to do something that sucks every day to have success, so do it early in the day.

I still don't get it right all the time.

As a gifted kid, I was brainwashed in the cult of perfection that anything less than 100% was a failure. As an athlete, I adopted this mentality, and it pushed me to excellence but reinforced my unreasonable standards of myself, a benchmark that often makes me "too much" to others because I demand excellence of myself and expect those that I surround myself with to put forth maximum effort frequently. That all you have to do is suck it up and go, and it will all work out.

As one of my former partners said: *I'm not you. I don't want to work that hard.*

And I didn't want them to be me, especially not the idealized illusion. But I did want them to be a better version of themselves instead of the worst version they became through laziness (mental, emotional, and physical). Sitting back on previous achievements is a path to degeneration. I rarely sit back and enjoy what I've done because I want to be Tony Stark, but I'm not. Nor will I ever be, but I can strive to be and adopt some of his better aspects while avoiding his worst. I can be better than my worst even if I do not reach my best every day.

Some days are rough. We all get beaten down by that client who decides to listen to uninformed and biased advice from an unqualified individual and decides not to listen to us as the expert (then gets angry at us when things obviously don't work out). By the daily grind of doing what we know it takes to build a business, with little or no positive feedback, we do the little things right over and over and without any accolades or production appearing. By the weather, and once again, the kids are on remote learning for the week. All the pressures, the little friction in our well-oiled machine that could bring it to a screeching halt.

And most days, we push onward and through. We slog on, doing what we need to do, looking forward to that rest and respite down the road. Sometimes we mentally check out for a few minutes and see ourselves on the beach in Tahiti with blue water and a drink, swinging in the hammock to the breeze. Once in a while, it is fantasizing about just throwing the computer out the window (defenestration, my second favorite word, by the way) or dowsing those reports in gasoline and striking a match. We've all been there, taking those little moments of escapism to deal with the all-too-real reality.

And then we get back to work, doing what we must do.

I'm not perfect. You're not perfect. The world and people can suck. Emperor Marcus Aurelius reminded himself of this every morning. He focused on doing his best at the task, which worked well most of the time.

Not everything goes right. In fact, most things don't. We all wish that our kids would pick up their room or do the chores even a quarter of the time we ask, that our favorite baseball player could get a hit even a third of the time and that even half the clients would listen to us.

So, I can't be perfect, as much as it gnaws at me. Every day is not rainbows, and six introductions and leprechauns bring me pots of gold and Guinness while riding T Rexes decked out for the Yankees Championship parade after I write the greatest love poem ever. Some days carry the weight of the world and expectations while slogging through the swamps of despair and faking a smile. Once in a while, it's "screw it," and doing the bare minimum and escaping to that beach in Tahiti for long stretches in my mind and eating cupcakes.

Just do the best you can, as often as you can. If I can do what I am supposed to do 90% of the day, I'll hit my goals and have a great month and year. So, I try my best to do what I need today and set it up so I can do it tomorrow, too. Not every day is perfect or even good. But if most of them can be pretty good, we're all doing ok.

And that's all right, even if we drop one of the chainsaws.

Right Thing

Do the right thing. Avoid the wrong choice.

Even if it makes you uncomfortable.

Resiliency Defined

What is Resiliency?

Resiliency is the ability to focus on the mission instead of the means. It is the capability to switch from Plan A to Plan B or C (even down to Plan Z if need be) to achieve the goal by whatever methods are needed without violating the ethical standards you live by.

Client X doesn't want to buy. Be ready to ask Y and # and σ and Q. No single case or client can make or break your production goals. Keep selling.

What if the power goes out? Not depending upon any single tool, deal, or person is a hallmark of resiliency. You need to be as ready to help a client with the whiteboard in your office or a napkin and pen as your high-powered, high-priced software. Mastery of your craft and confidence in yourself are components of resiliency.

The assistant calls in sick. What is your backup plan? A pinch hitter from an agency? Use technology? Do it yourself, even if not as efficiently for a little bit. Cross-train other staff members to step in? How do you make sure that day is not wasted if part of your team is unavailable? Independence is part of resiliency.

And what if they are not coming back? How do you replace them? How do you replace yourself if need be? As Charles de Gaulle said: *the cemetery is full of irreplaceable men.* How do you complete the mission even if you are sidelined, promoted out of the field, or on vacation? How do you make yourself replaceable? Subsuming your ego to the vision and mission is critical to resiliency.

The car tire is flat, or Corona cancels that conference. Cut off by an idiot driver and spill coffee on your suit? Do you harbor anger and resentment, or do you say "c'est la vie", and look for the upside, the hidden reason to laugh at the absurdity of the situation? Humor (especially dark humor) is a key to resiliency.

Resiliency is like water. It flows, adapts, and changes yet remains the same. It moves towards its goal around and over and through even mountains worldwide. It can be boiled or frozen and returned to its fluid state to continue the journey. As the resilient Bruce Lee said: *Be like water.*

Failure is Not an Option Burn the ships.

"Do, or do not. There is no try." Yoda Let me tell you a story. Some may say it is a myth or an urban legend. But I know it is true because I talked to the man and got the story straight from the source. I am not bragging; I am just stating a fact, like "the sun rose today." To him, the stuff of legend was merely doing what he needed to do.

This is a tale of Sam "The Man" Hazleton. Actually, Samuel H Hazleton IV, but still Sam the Man.

For twenty years before I entered the business, Sam was a "Top of the Table" (TOT) producer, earning roughly a million in production annually in today's dollars, often leading his entire company in Albany, NY. The 50th best market opportunity in the country, and he produced over a million dollars a year in premium in today's dollars, year in and year out, on 250+ lives with one assistant and his burning desire.

Sam did this by showing up every day and doing what he needed to do. He had played football at The University of Michigan, so he learned to practice hard and never take a play (or a day) off.

So, the myth is that Sam was seen walking down Central Avenue on a Friday evening, knocking on the doors of businesses and trying to talk to the owners because he hadn't hit his minimal weekly sales activity threshold. Sam had it ingrained in him that he had to see 15 people a week to hit his goals, and he refused to go home until he had done so. So, Friday, 5:30 on a cold and snowy, dreary upstate New York evening, Sam was still working, out in the cold, trying to meet people because he hadn't met 15 people and told them about what he did as of that point.

He could have been out with friends having a beer. He could have gone home. He was already a Lifetime MDRT member, repeatedly leading the Agency in lives and premiums, and well on his way to being a historically great producer. But he didn't go home.

He hadn't finished his week. He still needed to get 15 appointments kept, or else he had failed to do his job. And failure was not an option.

I asked Sam about the legend at one point after I had made MDRT.

He only smiled and said, "I saw my 15."

Do you refuse to go home until the job is done every day?

Do you get 5 plus introductions a day, regardless of weather or cancelations? You have the tools; do you have the desire?

Is good, good enough for you? Or do you need to be great to achieve that victory every day, no matter how you feel or what the world throws at you?

Just like Sam, you can't control if an appointment is kept, but you can control your reaction and actions. You can tolerate "almost" or refuse to accept from yourself anything less than your threshold for excellence every day.

Appointments canceled? Pick up the phone and call your best clients and tell them, "I can't go home until I get five introductions today. If you were in the same spot, who would you call?" Three calls, 20 minutes max, and your day will flip from failure to success so you can go home with a smile like Sam.

Do. Or do not.

Failure is not an option.

Resiliency

What made Edison great? His stick-to-it-ness after failures.

It is the same thing that made Bruce Lee into The Dragon: his ability to recover from a broken back and broken spirit, rebuilding body and heart into the indomitable icon.

The same thing that created Milton Hershey's iconic candy bar after multiple bankruptcies.

Or made our 16th President, Abraham Lincoln, a career failed politician, into the savior of the Nation.

Do you see the theme?

Dr. Lucy Hone's TED Talk, entitled "3 Secrets of Resilient People", in Christchurch, explains what makes resilient people succeed: they know the world is shit, but it isn't going to break them. They pick their battles and can let the non-core issues go. They know it isn't all shiny Instagram unicorns and fluffy clouds, but they find rainbows among the storms to make it through the hardest days. She had taught resiliency to soldiers, but then she had to live it: her 12-year-old daughter was killed in a car accident.

Admiral Stockdale's Paradox of survival in the Vietnam POW camps: *"You must never confuse faith that you will prevail in the end —which you can never afford to lose —with the discipline to confront the most brutal facts of your current reality, whatever they might be."* ~ James Stockdale In "Man's Search for Meaning," Viktor Frankl discusses pausing while slaving away in the concentration camps to stare at the beauty of the sun breaking from behind the clouds, of God's grandeur in the bleakest situation, and making it through another minute and another. After the horror, he was different but alive and adaptable in a way he would never have comprehended beforehand. He was resilient.

Balancing difficulties with belief in the future is the core of this resilience. Being pushed to or past limits without losing the core belief systems, without losing hope while "embracing the suck," as many military veterans describe it. Their dark humor might be a coping mechanism, yet they aren't giving up the fight that many still carry, and each day, they need to find a way to survive and win that day. Resilient.

[The Science of Resilience](#) from Harvard's Center on the Developing Child's YouTube channel consolidates millions of hours of research into a few minutes of scientific insight. You should watch it and ask yourself: How can I balance hope and what is currently occurring? How can I adapt and overcome?

As a martial artist, I repeatedly dealt with "career-ending" injuries, though none as severe as Bruce Lee's broken back. I was told I'd never be the same or compete at the same level. And yet I would come back smarter, tougher, better, more resilient, a champion.

The only career-ending injury is breaking your spirit.

If you can become resilient, you cannot fail. Because failure only happens when you don't get back up after being knocked down again.

"Nobody hits as hard as life," Rocky Balboa proclaimed. But you get up and keep fighting, *"and that's how winning is done."*

You might not go bankrupt multiple times like Hershey or fail ten thousand times like Edison. But if you refuse to lay down when you are hurt and keep going through Hell, growing, changing, and fighting, you can start to win and become unstoppable.

Because you are Resilient.

Limited Beliefs

Most people operate well below maximum capacity, whether in their business, physical performance, or relationships. For almost everyone, these are self-imposed limitations. We can only rise to the level of our beliefs; the ceilings we bump against are of our creation.

Our bodies are capable of much more than we let them do. Four-minute mile? Once thought impossible, yet now broken by high schoolers regularly. It was believed a marathon would kill a woman, yet last year almost 11,000 finished the Boston Marathon.

Broken spine? Former NFL star Ryan Shazier wasn't done.

Overcoming seemingly overwhelming odds extends to the business world all the time. Ben Feldman did not look like nor sound like an insurance agent. He had a lisp, was chubby, and suffered from social anxiety. Yet, for decades, he outsold most insurance companies and will forever be known as "The Greatest Life Insurance Salesman in the World." Like Babe Ruth of Rate Books, he set astounding production records that still blow the mind.

How about being homeless with a two-year-old child and becoming a billionaire? John Paul DeJoria did it.

JK Rowling lived on the dole but believed in her story of a young boy living below the stairs. Harry Potter is now the best-selling book series in history.

Don Chang emigrated from South Korea with almost nothing and poor English. He worked as a janitor. As the founder of Forever 21, he is worth over $6B.

What do they all have in common?

Belief—a driving, burning belief that makes obstacles irrelevant. That which stops others is just something else for them to get through because nothing will prevent them from making that vision a reality.

"Within me burns a flame which has been passed from generations uncounted, and its heat is a constant irritation to my spirit to become better than I am, and I will." Proclaims Og Mandino in *The Greatest Salesman in the World*.

"Don't quit. Suffer now and live the rest of your life as a Champion." Mohammed Ali.

"I make of myself a sacrifice to myself." Odin as he hung on The World Tree for nine days, trading his life for wisdom.

Be better.

Get out of bed and feed your mind and soul before feeding your body.

Listen to a motivational video while you work out, even for five minutes, while the rest of the world sleeps. Because Champions are made in the dark as Ali said, and he was and is The Greatest.

Set BHAGS (Big Hairy Audacious Goals) and post them where you can see them but no one outside your inner circle can.

Start busting your butt to achieve greatness without anyone seeing the change coming.

Practice your fundamentals every day, from asking for Introductions to asking for the business.

Practice with a purpose to perform perfectly.

Hunger for excellence instead of attention or accolades. Care about getting better instead of what others say because haters will hate, especially those who love what they do and are willing to leave small minds behind in the pursuit of greatness.

Stop thinking small.

Believe.

Know that you can bust through those limits and fly.

"A people without a vision will perish."

- The Book of Proverbs.

Believe and achieve.

Swim Like the Sharks

Sharks need to swim to survive. The forward motion pushes the water across their gills, which take the life-preserving oxygen for their metabolic processes.

If they stop, they will die.

Be a shark.

Don't sit and wait for the client to come to you.

Go to the client.

Don't wait for good things to happen; make them happen.

Pick up the phone. Send the email.

Sharks have no fear; they move forward and go after their next meal.

They don't look for motivation because they are motivated.

Action destroys fear.

Doing gets results.

"Bias for action," as Jocko Willink says. Move.

See target, attack target.

Just Do It.

If you are going through Hell, keep on going.

Onward.

Vamanos.

GO!

The Successful Psychopath

Imagine where you could be in your career ten years from now. Think about the new car you are driving, the tailored clothes, and the staff doing the paperwork so that you can go and do the face time with clients that are generating thousands if not tens of thousands, of revenue for you every single day. Feel the leather of your seat, the heaviness of the ring on your finger, and the watch on your right wrist. It feels good, doesn't it? Want to know what one thing will be most instrumental in getting you there?

Becoming a psychopath.

Hear me out before judging because I am going to make a case based upon decades of research by psychiatrists and neuroscientists that is informed by evolutionary biology as to why psychopathy could make you rich and successful. Suspend your assessments of the word and its connotations and be willing to explore the positive aspects and benefits of becoming immune to fear.

Our society has seen a dramatic increase in anxiety over the past few decades, with 2/5ths of new college graduates having received some form of counseling around stress management and reported negative effects from worry. The anxiety they feel is reasonable given the debt these recent grads carry and the not awesome job opportunities. The fact that this trepidation is hard-wired into most humans from our earliest day, back when being overly sensitive to the environment prevented us from getting killed by large dangerous animals or other early humans, is something we cannot escape. Our current over-stimulated world with lowered economic security and constant news feed of threats and danger certainly doesn't help and creates a situation that pushes many away from the financially uncertain world of sales (financial, real estate, etc.) because of the perceived risk.

But what if it didn't faze you? What if risk didn't bother you?

Imagine being hyper-alert but unconcerned and unafraid of the chaos.

Would being immune to the negative effects of the fearmongering of media and the constant stream of negativity help your career?

If you answered yes, you could start to see the advantage of a psychopath in the modern world. Not a Patrick Bannon, from the movie American Psycho type but one that is functional in society and has strong ethics. This could be the sixth dimension of OCEAN (Openness, Conscientiousness, Extroversion, Agreeableness, Neuroticism), or the five-factors personality typing. One who can remain cool under pressure, understand and predict the actions of the people they interact with, and can use cold, empathetic reasoning to make decisions that maximize outcomes. Someone conscientious, extroverted, and competitive is probably exactly what your hiring manager was looking for and your trainer attempts to reinforce, especially if you can easily say "next" and move on to the next potential client with strong self-confidence.

All tendencies of psychopaths.

Also, Presidents, JFK was near the high end of the psychopathic Presidential standards. Think about that, one of the most beloved Presidents has tendencies you'd attribute to Dexter or Hannibal Lecter.

The ability to manipulate others for your own benefit appears even more in CEOs than in convicted murderers. Controlling the potential downsides is the difference between a corner office and a cell.

What if you could build rapport with your clients and subtly maneuver them to help you develop your Introduction Based Business by becoming your fan? Is that psychopathy or good business?

Now, I believe you are starting to accept my thesis that adopting some of the mindsets of those considered on the spectrum of psychopathy might reduce some of your weaknesses in your practice.

"Who in the rainbow can draw the line where the violet tint ends and the orange tint begins? Distinctly we see the difference of the colors, but where exactly does the one first blend into the other? So, with sanity and insanity, "proclaimed Herman Melville in "Billy Budd". Push yourself along the spectrum, past your normal fear mechanism and restraint point. Not to daredevil level, but just a little more than where you were.

Then a little more.

It is a slippery slope with a positive result for your business as you become less worried about what others think. As your confidence builds and shows to clients and peers. A virtuous cycle, reinforcing your more aggressive tendencies that yield success.

No fear.

No doubt.

Supreme self-belief.

Come to the dark side and taste the success of the psychopath.

PARK

I was talking with some other Industry Leaders the other day about what it takes to succeed in our profession. This was an eclectic group from across the country, male and female, across two decades of age and numerous initial economic situations and ethnicities. Then the thoughts from our discussions marinated for a few days before popping out of my weird brain after a workout.

As a scientist, I like models and acronyms, and as a poet, I like things that represent larger concepts and lead to personal interpolation. So, the core concepts of success in business, be it financial advising, real estate, or coaching, are all concentrated in PARK.

Pride **A**ction **R**esilience **K**arma **Pride** is something I see misrepresented more and more in recent years. I don't mean the pride of the athlete who expects special treatment because they are freakishly gifted in some capacity (the same applies to nerds, by the way), but the professional pride of doing your best in every situation. Be it shoveling the walkway for the fifth time after a snowstorm or meeting with a client, putting your name and reputation on the line in each thing you do because YOU are doing it, and you expect to put forth maximum effort every time. Because that is what professionals do: their best every single time, in the big things and the mundane, they do all the pre-work to make certain no detail is missed, and they exert their will and energy to be as close to perfect as possible in everything they touch.

This isn't to say a professional is always feeling great, bright, and chipper and living on rainbow clouds with unicorns while they wear their rose-colored glasses. It does mean they don't take days off, that they know their mission is more important than how they feel. They know that every meeting is critical for the people that they serve. That they do the prep work and give their maximum effort for every client every time. There is a story of the Yankee Clipper, the spectacular DiMaggio not feeling well but still going out on the hallowed grounds of Yankees' Stadium and giving his all because *"some kid in the stands, this is their one chance to see me play."* He felt he owed himself, every iota of his ability, to those who paid to see him. Where have you gone, Joe DiMaggio?

Take Pride in what you do and constantly do it to the best of your capabilities. This alone could make you more successful than you ever dreamed possible.

Action is actually doing—not sitting, not thinking, not waiting—making things happen. It is movement that ultimately encourages motivation. Jocko Willink talks about a bias for action, and numerous therapist friends talk about taking that first step to move in the right direction. Take the first step, and the next, and the next.

Those who succeed don't count on things happening; they MAKE things happen. They don't just throw up a website or create content and hope to go viral. They grind, they push. They **do**, be it picking up the phone repeatedly, sending emails, or actually going out and shaking hands and handing their business card to people. They know that the hardest part is starting, so they keep going until they overcome the second hardest part of anything: finishing. They do what they have to do what they want.

Laziness will never lead to success.

Work your butt off, real work that moves you in the direction of your goals.

Action: GO!

Now **Resilience** is the biggest differentiator I've found. Call it grit, stick-to-it-ness, finishing the job, working through or around obstacles. I don't care what name you use or how you describe it, the mindset of never being licked, of figuring out some way to overcome objectives, to solve the problem no matter the constraints. Great start-ups make do in a garage with no funding and only brains, pluck, and creativity with the will to win.

When I get knocked down, I get up again.

Fall down seven times, rise up eight.

I'm not dead, so I haven't lost.

I refuse to lose.

"Because I said I would." Alex Sheen.

"Rock bottom became the solid foundation in which I rebuilt my life." JK Rowling.

You earn the good times if you can gut out the bad times.

If you're going through Hell, keep on going. Survive long enough to find a way to win.

Resilience: it's about willpower, not "won't" power!

And **Karma**? The cosmic wheel will rotate, returning to all what they gave to the universe.

As you sow, shall you reap.

"Givers get" per the Rotarians.

Do good to do well.

Work with gladness in your heart for the opportunity, be it in the corner office or the mailroom. Share a smile with others because it costs nothing to brighten someone else's day. Do what is right even if no one will ever know otherwise because it is the intrinsically correct thing to do. YOU will know, thus subconsciously influencing your future actions and interactions. Help someone out in some way, even if you have limited resources. Pay it forward because integrity echoes and resounds in the market and the halls of eternity. We teach the Cub Scouts to "do a good turn daily", and focusing on assisting others will lessen your own burdens and allow you to operate more freely. Serving the greater good in whatever way works for you will enrich your life and be returned to you in some capacity at some point.

Essentially every major world religion has a variation of The Golden Rule. Living this law, putting the Team before Self and Others instead of I, is an attitude that is more than prevalent among the truly successful in sports and business. Servant leaders know that they will be ok and sleep well at night by doing the right things. Helping others helps them.

What goes around comes around.

Karma is not a bitch. Karma is just and powerful. You should be too.

So that's it. PARK. Pride, Action, Resilience, Karma. The four components of sustainable success in any endeavor. All areas that we can all improve upon are competencies that we can develop through work and coaching if we truly desire to succeed and are willing to make the little sacrifices to achieve the great rewards that await.

Space Race

It was a time of tension in the US, and we were striving against a foreign power in proxy wars all across the globe and in a grander, non-combat theater for world leadership. The Space Race was in full effect, and the old methodologies and technologies were unsuitable for the new environment so far above the Earth. Yet even in this unprecedented advancement, some basic needs never disappeared.

Food.

Shelter.

Medicine.

Writing.

Beyond our atmosphere, all of these are critical. Even in space, things needed to be written, and the old way of doing things became dangerous to the mission.

The anecdote that NASA spent millions to develop a pen, and the Russians just used a pencil is a nice story about waste versus frugality, but it is completely false. Pencil lead is actually graphite, an isomer of carbon that is highly flammable and not exactly suited for a space vehicle. Traditional ballpoint pens are gravity-fed, so they fail in zero-G environments, too. A solution needed to be created.

No, the government did not pay millions to develop a "space pen". It was not centralized planning or the US Government that solved this problem. It was a small private company that developed a solution that worked in the extremes of space: microgravity, vacuum, insane cold, and intense solar radiation unfiltered by the atmosphere. For $2.39 each ($22.67 in 2024 dollars), the Fischer Space Pen was effective and safe and is even available to individuals today.

Today is like those times: wars, recessions, political strife, social inequality, business concerns, and economic fears.

Don't count on centralized planning to come and give you the tools you need.

Nor the government.

Look to the innovators, the experts devoting their souls to solving specific problems you encounter in your mission. These will provide you with the individual tools that cost-effectively get you what you need to get you where you are going, be it MDRT or beyond. Invest in yourself so that you can solve the problems you will inevitably encounter, and do not be afraid to challenge the existing thinking and try something different.

Or just be stuck on the ground, looking up at the stars and wondering why others can reach them.

Do Not Lie

Don't lie to others because it will become a habit. It will deteriorate and get worse and worse, a slippery slope, and eventually, you will get caught like a Fly in a Spider's web.

"Oh, what a tangled web we weave when first we seek to deceive."

More fundamentally, don't lie to yourself.

If you are honest with yourself, you will be honest with others.

If you tell yourself the Truth, the brutally honest truth, you can correct things in your life, whether at work or with your health, finances, or relationships.

Look in the mirror.

Look right into your own eyes. Look right into your own eyes, stare into your soul unflinchingly.

Do you like what you see? Or are there voids?

If there are empty spots or black holes, then look right into them. Acknowledge them.

DO NOT look away.

What is not right?

Be honest with yourself. Now you can work on correcting things.

Because you have stopped lying to yourself.

Change Versus Continuity

General and former National Security Advisor HR McMaster, in his book "Battlegrounds," mentions the two conflicting forces of change and consistency: diametrically opposed concepts that must be balanced to successfully fight a war. This embracing of antagonistic ideals is critical for success in business and life in general, too, and should be explored occasionally to expand our thinking and deepen our understanding of self, which is one of the most critical factors for those who give guidance for a living.

The world today is not the world of Alexander the Great or Marcus Aurelius or Ben Franklin or when we were kids, and yet it is also fundamentally the same in more ways than we want to admit in our egalitarian and technologically driven evolution. Two thousand years ago, Aurelius said, *"Today you shall meet with meddling, ingratitude, insolence, treachery, slander, and selfishness"*. Today, you will encounter orders of magnitude more because of larger populations and greater interconnectivity of the economy, all enhanced by traditional and social media, giving the loudest and most extreme a disproportionate power of influence. Ben Franklin's own grandson ran a slanderous newspaper that spread lies and deceit through the early years of the United States, maliciously and falsely spreading misinformation and attacking everything from how the yellow fever epidemic was handled to taxes to his own Grandfather.

The more things change, the more they stay the same.

McMaster first reached prominence beyond the battlefield for his book "Dereliction of Duty" (released in 1997 as an expansion of his Ph.D. Dissertation), which analyzed the flaws of leadership and logic that doomed the Vietnam War. The Afghanistan War supplanted Vietnam as the longest and most ineffective military campaign in US history for many of the exact same reasons he had discussed. Change is the only constant, but war remains brutal, and no matter how technology and tactics evolve, the fundamentals are the same as when the first tribe attacked another with fists and sticks.

We are still human.

We are still making the same mistakes as our great-great-grandparents, even with all the advancements in equality and employment and psychology and technology. When in business, someone says, "This time it's different" or "People have changed," without understanding simultaneously why they have NOT, I shudder and roll my eyes and go back to the Dot Com era or the Roaring '20s or the conquest of the Americas because we don't change, no matter how much we do.

People still take the easy route instead of the right one which is harder, takes more discipline with fewer guarantees, and does not give instant gratification. We now understand the biochemical mechanisms behind this, yet people still lie and cheat to feel good at the moment instead of feeling better long term, just as they did in ancient Greece or Rome or Civil War era America. The same yet different because the mechanisms and methodologies are more effective in some ways, but people are still essentially the same as we were five thousand or five hundred or five years ago.

Technology enhances people, for good and for bad. It does not change us even if it changes the world around us and how we interact with it and each other. Under the Snapchat filters, we are still the beautifully flawed and scarred people we were, and seeing the angel and devil simultaneously is the sign of emotionally and intellectually mature decision-making—the sort of decisions that lead to victory.

The analogy that business is war (as is love) is as ancient as commerce for a reason. It is a less bloody exchange but still on the spectrum of human interactions, of new innovations (Bitcoin or two bits or buck skin in exchange for food), allowing the most basic of human needs (food, shelter, water, safety) to be procured, thus hopefully allowing us to move up the pyramidic Maslow's Hierarchy of Needs. How we move up after meeting the basic needs has changed, but those basic needs are the same as in the past and will remain so in the future. Because we are human with the balancing forces of order and chaos within us. Whether Lover, Friend, or Foe, across the centuries, our needs are still the same; our base desires and lofty ideals remain consistent even though how we achieve them continuously changes.

And remember: the greatest war you will ever fight, your most difficult battleground, is not against an external opponent but internally between your past and your potential. Consistency and change in one human are a microcosm of all of us. Think about that.

Thankful 2

I am thankful for the chance to help other people every day.

I am thankful for the blue skies, the rain, and even the snow.

I am thankful for my family, even when they drive me insane.

I am thankful for those that help me or hurt me and make me grow.

I am thankful for shadows as they accentuate the light, and I am thankful for the dark sacred night.

I am thankful for everything I have ever been through,

And most of all, I am thankful for you.

Just Today

Just today, can you push yourself?

Just today, can you make yourself a little bit uncomfortable by calling one person you don't feel comfortable reaching out to?

Just today, can you put in that extra effort of preparation for your meetings this week so you are you more ready and can you deliver more of your professional promise?

Not always, but can you have one (just one) moment of doubt today where you take a deep breath and go forward, trusting that even though you are afraid, it is the right thing for your client (and ultimately for you)?

Not every day. Just today.

Today expand your personal emotional risk tolerance just slightly.

Just today, expand your envelope of comfort a teeny tiny bit.

Can you do that?

Then do it again.

And again.

And again.

Incremental miniscule gains create a tremendous future.

So just today, can you....

Rest

Sometimes you just need to rest. So, you don't break.

Recovery takes a lot longer if you don't do preventative maintenance.

It's like sending the kids back to school after summer vacation, and you close the door and enjoy the silence for a few minutes after the chaos.

After running an ultramarathon, my body doc (Dr. Baaden, aka "Magic Hands") forbade me from running for a week or lifting for several days so I could heal and recuperate. Given all the work she's done putting me back together, I follow the doctor's orders to rest and let time work its magic.

If you work hard (as opposed to hardly working or filling your day with busy work instead of productive activities) and are exhausted day after day from pushing yourself, schedule a day off. Maybe away from your kids, especially if they are as draining as mine. Maybe from your spouse, too, if you need a straight-up "me day" for your physical and/or mental health. Look in your calendar and find one day in the next three weeks that you can disappear and take care of yourself.

Maybe you've been pushing yourself to study for that licensing exam. I took two days after I passed the CFP® exam because I had been studying to the point the exam was cake, but I was still fried. Let your brain rest.

The day after I finished my book Every Day Excellence (I wrote 3-6 pages a day for almost six months on end), I literally wrote nothing but love poetry for the next several days and had to remind myself, "No, I don't have to write this morning!" The break was well worth it.

Push yourself as hard as you can, but schedule time off from it. Overtraining is dangerous for athletes and white-collar professionals, too. Rest will improve your performance and productivity when you return.

Muscles grow not when stressed while lifting but during recovery.

Neurons are enhanced not during the effort of learning but in the sleep that happens after.

Rest so that you can be your best.

I Failed

Today, I closed my Fraternity forever.

I took down the Charter, which was hung ninety years ago, with the names of the young men who chose to forge their destiny and build something new. That took risks and built something.

This organization produced Generals and Admirals, small business Founders, and Fortune 500 CEOs. It was created by architects, writers, engineers, and future billionaires. But most of all, it created leaders and thinkers, good men who would be fathers and uncles and set the example for future generations.

What happened?

Yes, some external circumstances may have accelerated the last stages of their fall. But in the end, the end came about because of one thing: a decline in standards.

Jocko Willink talks about holding the line, not giving in one iota on our personal integrity and excellence. We as leaders must coach and inspire the next generation to always do our best and strive to improve because we are modeling this in our actions and interactions.

This is where we failed. I say we because I, too, was complicit in the decline and fall.

Even holding myself to the highest personal standards, I failed to pass those standards on properly. I insisted that those who came after had a similar vision to that which fired me and made me desire to be better every day, to work, sacrifice, and grow on multiple levels. To build my technical and professional skills, I need to communicate what and why, coach and guide in addition to doing.

I failed these young men and the future ones who will not have the opportunities to learn what I did, to have the cradle of leadership rocked for them by those who came before and build off the foundations previously laid for their personal and professional development. These and all that could come after losing out on the chance to be part of something stretching back almost a century, to have the potential to build into the next decade and century something holding the core of the old and evolving with the world to be better. Bigger. Brighter. A lamp of excellence that helps them as individuals and an organization shine, unlock their talents, and push them to excellence as it did me and others for generations before.

We failed as a group to enculturate the new members and make them hold the line.

They didn't even know about the line because we failed them as mentors.

And now the line that stretched back almost a century is broken.

John Maxwell claims that a leader's true measure is the leaders they train. Making the next generation better than we are what all parents, managers, and coaches should strive for, yet too often, we fail because we are too busy doing instead of teaching. Take the time to execute your plan for greatness and create a legacy that lasts beyond your time.

Do not let your standards slip, whether in the office, the gym, or relationships. Hold fast to that vision of excellence and strive for it in all things, what the ancient Greeks called "arete." Constantly give your best and live with passion, but make sure the younger eyes see it and learn it and live it. Pass it on.

A Chapter closed.

Open a new one and write a brighter future by not just burning bright but lighting other lamps.

Go The Distance

I swore I would never do a marathon again.

I recently ran a double marathon (an ultramarathon) because two negatives are technically positives from a mathematics point of view. 52.5 miles, increasing in difficulty as I went way beyond anything I had ever done before and had to draw upon the reserves that I had accumulated in the months and years leading up to it by pushing my envelope to the edge of my comfort zone over and over and over again.

Only .5% of the population has done a marathon.

More people are doing ultras, a 3x increase since I did my first marathon in 2002. A little over 100,000 people a year do an ultramarathon, roughly 1.5 thousandths of a percent of the world population. Finding that number and typing it made me realize how crazy it is.

I did it.

Hitting the Top of the Table is about the same order of magnitude. Why not? It, too, requires daily discipline, having a supportive group of people that will cheer and abuse you, an absolute willingness to say "no" to things that won't help you reach your goal, and then guts. An unwillingness to give up and just grind it out step by step, meeting by meeting.

There are roughly the same number of Centimillionaires on earth as people who have done an ultramarathon. Think about that!

And know what? I HATE running. So does Ultrarunner David Goggins. But we do it because it makes us better.

I hate picking up the phone to make appointments. I get shakes before doing it, but I do it.

I hate paperwork with all the fury of an ADHD rebel Libertarian who rages against bureaucracy and inefficiency and just wants to get to work helping people, plus I remember when an app was eight pages and one signature instead of looking like War and Peace. Yet I still do it.

I run in the rain and cold, which I detest. They suck your energy away quicker than you can imagine. But I do it. Just like if you want to hit your BHAGS (Big Hairy Audacious Goals), you need to get out of bed and lace them up even if you don't want to work that day. Beautiful spring days call for golf or boat drinks or being outside instead of calling clients and solving problems, the same way freezing mornings call for staying under the covers. Accolades go to those with a strong dose of discipline that suck it up and do what they must.

At mile 40, I said, "I could quit; this is all I committed to." Then, that voice that drives me to excellence said, *"If you quit now, you'll always be a quitter."* I did not quit.

Find that voice that drives you to do crazy things because that is where excellence lives. Let average people have average lives; choose to be exceptional.

Go the extra mile.

Or 50+.

Blunt

Look, I'm not going to blow smoke up your butt and tell you the world is all rainbows and unicorns bringing bags of money right now. It sucks.

Lockdown is hard, especially if your business was built on direct contact and you used touch as a sales tool. And if you have kids at home like I do now, it is even worse.

Time to earn your money. You are in financial services. You don't deserve the finances if you don't provide the service.

Go and help the people.

Put on your uniform and get to work helping others.

Be the light in the world that is needed now.

Now

Now is the time.

Now is the time to turn uncertainty into opportunity.

If you are afraid, your clients are ten times more so.

Reach out and be the voice of reason to them in uncertain times.

That is what they want and need.

And others do too.

Every one of your clients knows people who are afraid and need guidance.

Ask them for the opportunity to help their friends, neighbors, and family, who are expressing concern and worse about what is happening in the world and are practically begging for your service.

Ask.

Show your leadership now.

Nice Guys Finish Last

It's time for some tough love. Know why you don't get enough introductions each week to make your business hum like a machine? Because you are too nice.

"It didn't feel right at the time" is an excuse used to avoid potential rejection of that other person saying, "No, I don't like you enough to introduce you to other people." So instead of being potentially confrontational and having a tough love, heart-to-heart conversation with the other person about honoring their word to introduce you to others, you let them off the hook so that you appear as "the nice guy/lady." You wimped out because you would rather have a smiling fake face in front of you than be real with them and earn their respect because that takes effort and carries risk.

Don't be nice.

Be respectful, always be respectful.

But don't let others push you around.

Be pleasantly persistent. Not a jerk, but hold your ground because you deserve the introductions and earned them, and don't let them weasel out of paying you means that you value the false friendship of someone trying to screw you more than you value yourself as a professional.

Ouch, right in the feels.

Too bad, there's more.

Every relationship, even a strong partnership, has an alpha and a beta at any moment—a wingman and a lead. Even if equal, like a marriage, there is a division of responsibilities, and one is more dominant in certain areas than the other because that is how the world works. In your business relationships, are you Batman or Robin? Are you the hero or the sidekick?

Clients need you to step up and lead them. They don't go to their doctor and say, "I'm in charge; I want Percocet." They don't go to their lawyer and state, "I screwed up, but here is how we are going to fix it." So why do you let them tell you how to run your business?

If a client doesn't introduce you to others when they agreed to, and you LET THEM DO THAT, you are laying your ego on the ground, proclaiming, "Please wipe your feet on me because I am your doormat."

Do you let them doubt you more than you believe in yourself? If so, you need to either strengthen your belief or find a different profession because you will be miserable.

Don't let them step on you or use you.

Stand up for yourself and your values.

Believe.

Or wuss out like you have been.

Pack your cubicle up because it is "when you leave this career," not "if."

Grow a backbone, know you created value, and insist on being paid for your time with quality referrals.

Pack up and leave, or plant your foot and say, "No. I deserve these."

Are you going to take flight or fight?

Instead of platitudes, get some attitude and don't be bullied.

Because nice guys do finish last.

One Warrior

Heraclitus observed 2,500 years ago that of every 100 people entering battle, 90 were useless. 9 were the real fighters who would hold the line of the battle. But the One Warrior would turn the tide and snatch victory and glory. David Goggins discusses this in the introduction of "Can't Hurt Me" and how he went from an illiterate 297-pound cockroach spraying failure to *"the baddest man God ever created."* Through his own efforts (like Nietzsche's Übermensch), he became the One Warrior.

Are you The One?

Becoming The One is more about mindset than natural gifts. Yes, you must have base-level acumen and physical gifts (a five-foot-five person probably does not make the NBA, no matter how many hours they spend in the gym). As Malcolm Gladwell pointed out, intense, focused practice with a purpose will carry an average, talented individual to success, making them one of the nine who can hold the line. Being in the top 10% is not bad at all; it will make you the envy of others who are unwilling to sacrifice time as you have. But to become the 10% of the 10%, The One, takes more than a single type of sacrifice. It requires you to make a sacrifice for yourself. Like a phoenix, you must burn from within and scorch your weaknesses away to be reborn better.

To be The One, you must be willing to purposely break yourself down in all dimensions: physically, mentally, and spiritually. To be The One, you must have the passion and discipline to go where the other 99% won't: deep into yourself, into the dark areas of your past and your soul, and face the demons hiding there. To wrestle with and conquer them, subjugate them to your will and greater purpose. The nine fighters will occasionally confront their demons as they arise. The One will actively seek out the monsters within and harness their power. It is terrifying to do so, but The One repeatedly separates itself from others over time because it chooses to face these internal and external opponents.

"Once you know what you want, sacrifice everything to achieve it." Oishi

"My only rival is within." Ruelle

"Who looks outside dreams. Who looks inside awakes." Carl Jung The One will look inside for strength beyond what can be externally imposed. The great samurai Ronin Miyamoto Musashi taught that nothing external will make you greater, only what you have within that you develop, like the hammering and folding of the katana blade over and over and over until the impurities are removed. The different types of steel are integrated into a stronger, more flexible weapon that extends the wielder's spirit. Are you ready to hammer yourself repeatedly to remove your flaws, to draw out the bad things, and become a weapon of your soul, unstoppable in the battles you will face? That is the nature of The One.

The One continues to evolve because they know they are never done improving, that "good enough" is the start of a plateau and then decline instead of the constant climb up the mountain of excellence. The One applies James Clear's ideas of continuous compounding improvements from *Atomic*

Habits, the same concept Jim Collins calls the Flywheel in *Good to Great*. The daily refusal to step back and to even push ahead. There is always a little more inside, another rep in the gym, a mile on the road, or a call to be made. That little bit better today than yesterday as you develop your skills and will that the only days off are truly days off for rest and recovery, not half-assing it in the office or the gym and sort of working but not really. The One will push themselves harder in preparation than others in their performance, so when it is time to battle, they have more in reserve than others can comprehend. Think of Michael Jordan's performance with the flu or when he sensed victory. Are you willing to make the hours and years of sacrifices in preparation for the fleeting moments of greatest glory? That is the mindset of The One.

The One will grind until they have removed the unnecessary surface impurities. As Bruce Lee focused on simplifying and eliminating, the One gets down to the essence, so the pretty, flashy, and showy extraneous is removed for the focus on function and efficient excellence, whether it is in a martial arts technique or a sales call. Kaizen applied to themselves and what they do.

Be the One. Work on yourself harder than you work on anything else, as Jim Rohn revealed decades ago. Know thyself and focus on improving the one person you can control: yourself. Dedicate yourself today to be the best you possibly are next year and a decade from now, and you will become at least one of the nine. Eventually, you will look back over your victories and know what it feels like to be The One.

Donuts Or Do Nots

Donuts make me happy.

They do not make me fulfilled.

Running helps me develop the mindset and discipline to be fulfilled. It is an ongoing process of challenging myself. It does not make me happy, but it does let me eat donuts, which makes me happy.

Running ten miles when I do not want to builds my resolve for the things I need to do that I don't want to do. Think about your business: there are multiple things you probably hate doing almost as much as I hate running. Are you willing to do them consistently for an hour or two a day, every day, so that you can do all the other things you like to do in your position? Or are you having the donuts without earning the right to do so? Do not give in and cheat and get the reward without the work. It is unsustainable and ultimately unfulfilling.

A BMW won't make me happy. Doing the things to be able to buy a Beamer in cash will. Having the capability to do something but the discipline to not do it unless you EARN it and make a better selection is even more rewarding. The journey becomes the destination, the skills developed and sights along the way more valuable than the visible accolades at the end. This is more of an internal strength versus external gratification and validation mindset; overall, it will make you more fulfilled than cycling through flashy new vehicles (or clothes, or relationships) in an attempt to let the flashlight you instead of your internal fire powering and guiding you. If you focus on the work it takes to earn the trappings instead of the trappings themselves, you will be more fulfilled.

Choose to wait for the greater good, the better reward. Do the things to get there that make you develop excellence, and you can live a life of significance instead of convenience, a life of fulfillment instead of a life filled with stuff and cheap thrills that diminish your overall potential and legacy.

Do the miles and dials that others won't, and you can do things that they can't and can't even comprehend.

And along the way, you can still have the occasional donut.

Break Away

In cycling, the riders clump together in the pack of the peloton. Except for the champions: they break away from the pack and win the Yellow Jersey and the title.

In distance running, the goal is to have a kick and break away from the pack. Every mile matters: every step is a difference maker over the distance. But who has the reserves of emotion and strength at the end determines who breaks the tape and the records.

Break away.

Lead from the very front and push yourself against yourself instead of the other competitors. Don't look at them or what they do.

Celebrate your victories. You earned the accolades. But a celebration should take less time than the actual act of winning. Don't have a good day and take the next month off. Bask in the moment, then start working on your next win so that you recapture that fleeting moment of glory and ecstasy. Champions return to the gym immediately after they win because they are still starving for excellence and victory. They also know that the wolf on top of the mountain, at the pinnacle, is rarely as hungry as the one climbing the mountain.

Truly exceptional businesspeople and athletes are addicted to the rush of victory AND the grinding work needed to achieve it.

David Goggins was in the gym a few hours after a mission, and someone asked him why he wasn't resting and what was wrong with him. *"You will never understand what is wrong with me,"* he responded as he worked to improve.

Even when injured, Kobe Bryant would train and watch tapes to hone his skills. The Mamba Mentality was to look for an edge constantly; Human Kaizen applied to basketball and everything else he did to continuously improve even after hoisting the trophy.

Gravity draws bodies towards the largest masses. It takes focused energy to overcome this attraction, achieve escape velocity, reach orbit, and break away from the unseen bonds that hold us down.

Break away.

It takes effort to get out of bed at dark thirty and train. The Rock does it daily, as do I. Do you?

It takes willpower to consistently sacrifice going out with your buddies and instead go home and study for your CFP®, CCIM, or LLM. Break away from the pack mentality to do things they can't comprehend. Then, you can live the life they can only dream about because you deferred happiness and compounded it.

Average is a disappointment. Excellence should be your standard. 2nd place is the first loser.

Be different. Be better. Expect the best from yourself, and make the sacrifices to be the best you possible.

Break away from the underperformance of your past.

Be Better.

Break away.

I Will Fight

The enemy is at the gates, relentless and numberless in power.

Darkness of the soul creeps across the land as families huddle in fear.

Will you flee?

No.

I will fight.

I will fight though I may fail, for others will see and be inspired.

I will meet the enemy with courage and the strength of a hundred as I do right and protect others.

I will fight.

I will fight when others have abandoned hope.

I will fight for those who have abandoned hope.

I will fight, and I will bring hope against the Darkness. My light will burn and light the beacons.

I will fight.

Justify

Canadian psychologist and author Jordan Peterson declares, *"Make a life for yourself in three years that will justify the suffering."* Let's explore this.

Are you sitting there in mild uncomfortableness, where you don't like where you are but are unwilling to make changes? It's like the dog lying on the porch with a nail sticking up from the floorboards that's bothering her, and she's whining but doesn't get up and move because it doesn't bother her enough to do something about it. Get up and do something about your situation because the whining about it and the unwillingness to change is really annoying to others.

As The Dread Pirate Roberts tells Buttercup in "The Princess Bride": *"Life is pain, Highness. Anyone that says differently is selling something."* This is actually a man testing the love of his life that he risked death for (and actually overcomes being mostly dead for), who suffered on a pirate ship with the constant threat of death for three years, who fought a giant and survived torture for. Roberts (aka Wesley, the farm boy) justified his suffering for love, true love, and it transformed him.

Are you ready to let pain transform you into someone greater?

Many of my friends have built tech companies, and there is a constant in the successful ones: sacrifice for a dream. They take under-market compensation (or no payment at all to start and often skip paychecks in tough times), slave away for long hours (70 hours a week is generally the minimum to start) on complex problems that are ever-evolving, rarely have a social life (no time and too tired) and have to juggle a dozen different responsibilities so are forced to grow in numerous ways simultaneously. And they love the stress and pain needed to create something worthwhile, something they are proud of that employs dozens or hundreds of other people and positively impacts millions. That was justified suffering because they believed in the future more than the pain of the present and turned themselves from talented coders to great leaders. Are you ready to sacrifice your time, surface relationships, and your worst aspects to convert your potential to actual greatness, or are you going to suffer to make someone else reach their dreams while yours wither? That is needless suffering.

Are you ready to suffer to generate new business and get paid, or will you whine about having no money but be unwilling to do the work to correct this? Just like the dog on the porch, it hurts but not enough for you to get up and do something about it. Quit whining, get off the porch, and hunt!

Are you going to cold call hundreds of people a week to eke out a few sales and be stuck doing that week after week and year after year, with no change as you get beaten down and mentally exhausted from the constant hang-ups and abuse? Or are you willing to suffer the emotional risk and short-term time sacrifice to learn to ask for Introductions so that you can ween yourself off of cold calling, build an Introduction-Based Business, and have the life in three years that the effort justifies?

Athletes understand the sacrifices of time and fun and even acquaintances to invest their time to develop themselves. The pain from training, the recovery from injuries, the crushing emotions of losing, the early mornings and late nights, and the limited social life to become elite. To do things that others more naturally talented won't experience because they are unwilling to choose the pain of betterment and never make a better self and life for themselves. Athletes understand suffering as the price for excellence, and a championship justifies those early mornings and late nights and aches and pains.

Sports, business, and love all require a price to be paid for success; that price is time, pain, and part of your soul. Over time, all are worth the sacrifice, the bumps and bruises, the rough patches and emotional valleys to climb the mountains and see views others who are unwilling to struggle will never experience. As Madonna sang, "Justify your love", but more importantly, justify your pain and struggle by creating a life worthy of you and your sacrifices as you build something significant of and for your loves.

Ride Harder

If you smack a pile of wet rags, you make a noise and a mess and nothing else.

If you hit a wild animal, they will attack you and nothing good comes of it.

But if you whip a thoroughbred, they go faster and faster, pushing their limits.

Find someone to push you, whether internal or external, if you want to win the race.

Skill Set

I have studied martial arts for decades, since before The Karate Kid came out (not the one in China, the real one with Pat Morita as Mr. Miyagi). My martial arts skills consist of two main components: understanding and doing.

Understanding is exactly that: intellectual (and spiritual) reflection and study, whether it is the physics behind a long roundhouse kick or the physiology as to why to strike someone in the solar plexus (forget "a man can't stand, he can't fight", a person that can't breathe can't chase you and has fear instead of fury). This is where theory lives and experimentation to discover what works in the real world as opposed to movies or the "massless, frictionless" world of physics textbooks. The deep knowledge that takes years to develop, not an hour-long seminar, promises to turn you into the next Gracie or UFC sensation.

The other part is doing. Over and over and over. Repetition to the point of remembrance. I still throw the first technique I learned after how to bow (a horse stance center punch) 100+ times every morning with each hand. At this point, I have thrown over 10 MILLION punches in my life. I don't have to think about it; I can just do it.

I don't think about asking for Introductions anymore. I just do it. I am unconsciously competent in this skill at this point, but I still use some basic reinforcers like an agenda or a feeder list to ensure that I don't slip, the same way that my Tae Kwon Do Master still practices his basic techniques after 60 years. Good habits like practicing your fundamentals never go out of style. As Bruce Lee said: *I do not fear the man who has practiced 10,000 techniques, but the man who has practiced a single technique 10,000 times.*

Don't just read what is laid out here once and move on. Read and re-read. Reflect. Practice. Try it out (don't worry, no one is punching you in the face if you slip up), then reflect, practice, and try again. You don't become a guitar god or Fortnight champion without repetition and reflection, and you won't become an Introduction Machine without the same mindset.

And remember: you're not me. My one instructor, Master Bill Durkhee, reminded me that you're not me: be the best you possibly can be. He was 6'3", 195 lbs. of sinew and muscle, and called "The Machine." I was 160 lbs. and called "The Computer." I used and enhanced my natural gifts and strove to improve my weaknesses to become the best me I could. You should do the same based on your constraints and talents.

SKILL SET

Not An Act, But A Habit

"We are what we repeatedly do. Excellence, then, is not an act but a habit." No, not Aristotle as often attributed, but Will Durant summarizes Aristotle's core teachings in a manner more palatable to modern readers.

The translation does not change the facts and actually conveys the message better than the ancient Greek or the antiquated direct translations, much as related to the story of Caedmon in Latin and the transcription of dreams and languages losing their power. The best translations of The Tao Te Ching are not the truest to the text but capture the poetry of the thoughts. So, too, with our profession. Translate my ideas and words into your native tongue and style.

Al Granum created activity management (he called it Client Building) almost a century ago. Some of his verbiage has been updated (going from "suspects" to "Introductions" and "dials" becoming "attempts") reflecting the technological evolution, but in many ways, the narrow focus of his era needs to further expand into the current post-Glass-Stegall world, like physics evolved from Newtonian to Quantum and unleashed the entire world of technology. Mickey Straub has done so to Granum with SAMUSA (Sales Activity Management), and as our world continues to evolve, so will the tools used to build financial services careers. For example, we no longer use hand shovels to dig foundations to construct buildings, and nail guns have replaced hammers for most construction purposes. The old tools still make sense in many situations, but professionals know when to

169

upgrade the instruments of their craft. Yet the core of what they do is unchanged.

Hopefully, you have mastered your craft, like the builders of old and modern days. The core of what we did in 1921 was the same as in 1983 as today: help people build their futures by protecting them from the elements beyond their control. Not necessarily wind and rain and sun and animals but uncertainty, inflation, taxes, old age, and all the side effects of these. The goals are the same, even if the verbiage and methodologies have evolved.

Agents in the mid-1990s used rate books to calculate costs. Are you using the equivalent in your client acquisition process by using cold calls or mailers instead of email and social media? The rock-as-a-hammer approach works if you are on a deserted island and need to bang something out, but actually choosing to do so in our modern world is wasteful and ineffective.

The Master uses their tools until they are second nature but is also aware of improvements so that their craft can continue to improve at the pace of the world around them. Are you evolving via Shosen (the "Beginner's Mindset" of the various Japanese martial arts), or have you become arrogant in your mastery and positioned yourself to be outmoded because you no longer can grow?

The great artists continue to evolve over the decades. Picasso or Pitre. Johnny Cash. Morgan Freeman. Ben Feldman. They never forget the core of their profession and the skills they learned early, but they are never afraid to embrace the new so that they can bring their message to a wider audience.

While maintaining the habit of excellence, the self-imposed standards that created success instead of the other way around.

How are you evolving?

Client building, or sales activity management, is as true today as it was fifty years ago and will be true five decades from now: if you measure what matters and care about improving, better results will come. You can see this idea in your business, health, and personal life.

Excellence is a habit; however, you want to define it.

And so, be excellent today.

Week 1

It's the first week of the year. Granted, ANY week can be the first week of the best year of your career, but let's assume you are actually reading this at the start of an applicable calendar cycle for you.

Let's talk about how to set up your world to maximize your potential of blowing through your goals for the year, no matter what they are. Here are a handful of things I have had success with, as have many others I've worked with.

1. Weekly Goal.
    a. Take your overall goal (let's say $250k of production for calculations). Divide it by 50, because we will assume that you take two weeks off out of the 52 weeks in the year. Now increase that number by 10% (so in our example $250k/50 = $5k, plus 10% or $500 for $5,500 per week). This is your weekly goal. Why? Because stuff happens, whether a sick kid or getting a concussion playing softball or sick parents. Build in the "fudge factor" to have a margin of safety for things beyond your control.
    b. What weekly activity is required to generate this production? Break it down based on your own numbers (or company/industry standards if you are new or lack tracking numbers). How many times do you need to ask someone to buy? How many Introductions do you need to get in front of these people? How many times do you need to pick up the phone? Know the numbers to generate the activity

needed to hit your weekly goal. Then do what you need to do each week.

2. Calendar Control.
    a. Schedule practice time every morning. Every day, so your skill set continuously increases and sharpens.
    b. Schedule client acquisition time daily. Enough time to replicate the good days

where you are running sufficient activity to hit your weekly production goals.

    c. Schedule research time regularly. Book time at least a few times a week to research potential clients and build target lists. If you don't put this into your book, you will find a way to avoid it because it isn't fun, but it is necessary.
    d. Win early. Try to hit a third of your weekly activity goal on Monday so that you are mentally in the bonus round. And remember, win the morning, win the day (JRRT). If you can hit your daily goal before lunch, you will be operating in the bonus round for half the day and will be more effective.
    e. Rest. If you are running hard each week, you need some time off. If you plan ahead and hit your goals early in the week, there is no excuse not to schedule Friday afternoon off to recharge your batteries. And once a month, take a three-day weekend—just get all your production done in four days instead of five.

3. Proper fuel. You need the right fuel every day to run your machine.

Eat well. You need enough calories and high-quality ones as appropriate.

    a. Consume knowledge each day. Read, listen to audiobooks, watch YouTube videos—whatever works for you. Empty calories for your brain are as bad as empty calories for your belly.

    b. Emotions. You need love and friendship. Get some, whether it is your BFF sending you a meme to make you laugh or your crush sending you a smile. Hug from your kid or kiss from your significant other. You need a few helpings of positive emotions daily from people you care about.

    c. Feed your soul. Pray or meditate or whatever you personally do to connect with the greater Universe and grow in gratitude. Do this religiously (pun intended).

These actions require consistency week by week and day by day, but excellence is a habit, and sporadic efforts cannot achieve big goals.

"To be excellent, you have to be consistent." Me.

If you want to do something significant, break it down and do the little things each day to move you to business success and overall greatness.

IF/THEN

Computer programming is built around a simple statement based on Boolean logic: if x, then y. So simple, so elegant, and so powerful that you should adopt it in your financial advisory practice to get many more introductions and drive your production to MDRT and beyond.

This conditional logic is at the core of conditional contracting in the Sandler Sales system and aligns directly with the psychology of choice that led to Nobel Prizes in Economics for Thaler and Kahneman.

Applying this concept in your business is wicked simple: in your initial discussion with the potential client, just state the conditions: **IF** I create value for you in our meeting today, **THEN** you will introduce me to other people I should talk to about what I do and how I help people, the same way that So and So introduced us. Is that fair and reasonable?

Re-read that.

Let's analyze this from the end.

"Is that fair and reasonable" is my favorite phrase in all negotiations, whether it is sales or trying to convince an eight-year-old to do something they don't want to do. Because my proposals are always both, and the only way to dispute them is a non-emotional analysis of the merits of the proposal. The eight-year-old might say something is unfair, but if it is consistent with other expectations, this argument is quickly dismissed, even if your client is acting like the eight-year-old. Similarly, "reasonable" neutralizes emotions and forces the individual to make a mental calculation that dismisses fear and allows them to be guided to the conclusion that they wish by weighing the facts. So "is that fair and reasonable" can have only one outcome as long as you, as the Agent/Advisor, are a professional: yes. This is exactly the agreement you want for the verbal contract.

The section before "fair and reasonable" states "the same way So and So introduced us" and carries power because you are sitting with this person because of the introduction of another. If they had not introduced you, then you would not have had a conversation with this potential client. This allows you to harness herd mentality positively: this person will be ok introducing you to others because EVERYONE introduces you, and they want to be like everyone else.

By creating a valuable experience for this person in your initial meeting (by uncovering potential issues they can avoid, initiating valuable discussions on savings and investment philosophy, providing some basic education they might be missing, etc.), you then make the first part of the upfront contract, the IF/THEN statement, have only one outcome: yes, value was created.

If the answer to this question is ever No, explore with the person again what you discussed and get them to remember and highlight some of the points from the meeting that could be life-changing to them, whether it is suggesting they put away more for retirement as they are completely off track for that goal, or introducing them to other professionals that they need, or answering questions they had. They need to acknowledge that you have fulfilled your end of the bargain (add value) so that you have the right to their end, your payment with introductions to others that you should talk to the same way So and So introduced the two of you.

If the client finds no value in your meeting, I strongly suggest you review your process, initial meeting questions, and agenda. It could be a YOU problem.

But if you have the client agree to the verbal contract and deliver value so that the answer to the IF statement is a positive response, then the next logical step is they fulfill their end of the agreement because they have created a moral obligation within themselves. Most people will honor the bargain, and most that try to argue their way out of it are easily convinced to meet their obligation to you because of the social mores and principles of honor ingrained in most of us. Just stick with the facts instead of emotions: "IF I added value, THEN you would introduce me to others. You agreed that I created value. Therefore, you will introduce me to others as a person who keeps your word."

Ethical people will keep their word and fulfill their contract with you. Unethical people should not be accepted as clients because they will screw you and your staff over at some point. Use this verbal contract to gauge the potential client's commitment to the financial planning process and to weigh if they are a person of integrity.

It may seem weird to invoke computer logic as the basis of your client's payment and the foundation of your business relationship, but remember that the greatest computer ever created resides between your ears. If you program it properly, you will never have to worry about getting more than enough introductions for your business to thrive.

Perfect Practice
Perfects Performance

Practice will not improve your performance. Focused, intended, and intense practice will make you better, whether as a financial representative getting introductions or as an athlete or performer. But most people don't know HOW to practice unlocking their excellence.

First and foremost: game time is NOT practice time. When you are face to face with a client is not the time to try something new: it is time to implement something new. You should try it over and over in the bubble of your practice, a Dr. Strange-esque Mirror Dimension combined with Time Stone so you can fail over and over until you understand why, fix it, and do it right over and over again.

As the Hall of Famer Lenny Moore told my office: *amateurs do things until they get them right. Professionals do it until they can't do it wrong.* Are you an amateur or a professional?

In The Art of War, Sun Tzu proclaimed, *"The victorious General has fought the battle a thousand times in his palace ere he takes the field."*

Set aside time to practice every day. The easiest and quickest way is to dedicate your commute to the office to mental prep time. It does not matter if it is eight minutes or eighty; if you dedicate the ongoing commute time to honing your skills, sharpening your edge, and mastering your weapons, you WILL accelerate your development.

SKILL SET

So how do you maximize that time to augment your skill set?

First, sit down and write out your ideal language.

Not all of it. Even Mozart would not sit down and write an entire symphony at once. Choose a particular part of your language (the up-front contract with a client, or your transition into asking for your introductions, whatever is most glaring at the moment in terms of developmental needs) and write out what you should say (instead of what you probably actually do say).

Note, we want you to write it with paper and implement it, NOT type it on a computer or dictate it. WRITE it. Because of the haptic feedback, your muscle memory recognizes the words. You increase your retention by roughly 10% by writing something down (one trick you should apply with your clients by making them take notes in your meetings). Pressing buttons on a keyboard does not have the same effect.

After you write your language down, read it out loud to hear how it sounds. You will probably tweak it, adding phrases like "fair and reasonable" or directions like tapping your chest (as a psychological anchor) or what have you.

Read it out loud again and tweak it. Repeat.

Repeat.

Repeat until you are not tweaking it.

Now write it out. Now read it.

Write it. Read it. Again.

Repetition is needed to affix the imprint into your brain. You are reading it out loud to also develop muscle memory, so your body adapts to saying these phrases and your ear hears you saying it, as your own voice is powerful for memory encoding.

Now grab your cell phone.

Open a voice memo.

Read your language.

Save this memo and listen to it on your commute multiple times. Speak along with it. Mimic the perfect you.

And do this on off days, too, as champions have no days off.

Listen to it within a half hour before bed so that it is at the top of your mind for memory encoding as you drift off to sleep.

Do this every day for a month.

You will see a dramatic improvement in performance because you have intense, intended, and focused effort on a fundamental building block.

After a month, choose a different piece of language to focus on. But do not forget the one you were just enhancing because a tool becomes dull if not sharpened. Still, listen to that voice memo a few times a week, as the lower repetition with an established skill is okay to maintain as opposed to creating anew.

Repeat with a new piece the next month.

And the next.

If you were to do this for a year, how great would your development be?

What about over five years?

Champions are not made overnight. It takes years of work, of practice, of perfecting.

Practice prevents poor performance.

The perfect practice provides power.

Now get to work.

Process

"Anybody who is highly successful at what they do has a process," one of my closest friends told my son this weekend while he was working on his Engineering Merit Badge for Boy Scouts. And this guy is a GREAT engineer, the best I've ever met at getting large, complex systems to work right. He is spot on.

Successful writers usually have a process, be it working every day at the same time for a minimum amount of time, no matter how they feel or how they research their next book. They use their own language to tell stories that move the reader, often changing their perspective.

The Great Masters had an approach and process to painting, covering everything from sketching ideas to making their paintings. Those who used a systematic and repeatable technique produced multiple works of art that are canon. Excellence is not usually a hit-or-miss, throwing paint-against-the-wall mess (unless you are Jackson Pollock, who made it his signature style).

Great athletes have routines that help them get in the zone and produce. These routines aid them in getting the repetitions needed for excellence, and the Hall of Famers generally practiced harder than they needed to simulate game conditions and push their performance to the level of immortality.

What is your process to build an Introduction Based Business? Are you consistent with how you systematize your efforts, or are you sporadic and spastic in your production?

A consistent process, even if flawed, is better than winging it. Talent will top out without understanding and practice, and processes lead to the predictability of outcomes. Processes can be improved continuously, and lead to greater production.

If you don't have a process for continuously getting Introductions of the type you want and in the numbers that you need to achieve your goals, get one. Create it or steal it from someone else, just get one.

If you take another's process to build your business though, make sure you personalize it. Break it down into the steps, and make sure the steps are aligned with your personality type or else you will create internal friction that potential clients will easily see, and you will struggle. Better to be a decent (and improving) version of yourself than a bad knockoff of someone else. This book has not just excellent verbiage that has been successful for others, but the blueprint of how many top producers have structured their process for garnering Introductions. Steal it and tinker with it. Play with it. Understand the process thoroughly so that you can then alter it to fit you, before you master it.

Adopt an SOP, a Standard Operating Procedure. Even if not perfect, even if it is not done every time but merely most of the time, this is drastically better than just going by gut every time unless you are among the truly gifted. But those who go from Gifted to Great still have a process to maximize their abilities.

Improvement rarely happens by accident but with intent.

Companies spend billions a year improving their processes, because it results in billions more output and profit. Learn from them. Process leads to production and profit.

Natural Outcome

Success should be the natural outcome of planning and execution.

You should not be excited about hitting your goals if you developed the plan and did the work daily and weekly to achieve the production level you predicted. You should be excited for the daily activity, the individual meetings that build your business hourly and daily.

Love the process, not the outcome.

We can't have any particular case closed or any individual client buy with certainty. We can only influence the event. But as statistics tell us, we can predict overall outcomes with decent certainty. Statistical mechanics leaves very little to chance as the number of events becomes massive, just like actuarial science or, hopefully, your business.

You know your current ratios between Introduction, appointment, and Client. If you don't, either figure them out or look them up for your industry/office. Then, use these numbers to determine what you need to do in terms of activities you can control and influence to hit your goals.

If you know that one out of four times you ask someone to buy, they will do so on average, then you know that if you ask twelve times a week, you will, on average, get three sales for the week. Knowing that you get into a position to ask someone to buy from one out of every 2 initial meetings, you can interpolate that you need 24 meetings to achieve the twelve chances to ask the people to take action, yielding your three sales. Focus on getting the twenty-four or more meetings, five every day, because you can control how many attempts you make to set these appointments. That is 100% under your control. The three sales are under your influence only.

Focus on your daily and weekly activities that directly translate into business.

You control:

Number of attempts to set appointments.

Number of appointments set.

Asking for Introductions in every meeting.

What time you start your business day.

What you intake for education and motivation. Being respectful and kind to others.

How much you practice your language.

You only influence:

Number of appointments kept.

Your ratios.

Sales outcomes.

How others act/react.

Everyone expends energy (emotional, intellectual, physical, monetary) on things that they can influence, and often the most is expended where we have the least influence.

Focus on what you can control:

Get up early, work out, and feed your mind, body, and spirit with good stuff.

Practice your craft daily.

Start working early and give your best efforts. Treat people well.

Invest time in the most important activities and with the most important people.

Review the day, see what you can do to improve what you control or influence strongly

(usually through practice that improves skills in particular areas). Repeat.

Repeat.

If you fall in love with this process, the daily little things needed to lay the foundation of your future, you will continuously approach your goal. Yes, there will be curveballs like COVID-19, your car engine dying, or a kid getting sick. You can't control the questions on the test, but you can control how you prepare for it.

Outcomes are totally beyond your influence, and all you can do is focus on what you can control, how you approach your business and life, and finding ways to do the daily and weekly activity that you need to do no matter what the Universe decides to pull out of its bag of tricks this month. Sustainable success comes from embracing the Stoic belief of controlling your mindset and your actions and letting the world do what it will do.

So, focus on what you can control and do what you need to do daily; as the days and weeks go by, you will inevitably approach your goals in a repeatable and inevitable manner. Success is the reflection of your daily choices that determine your actions, so choose to do the daily investments of your time and energy to follow your plan for excellence.

SOP

The other day, I was wickedly busy and violated my own protocol: I did not check my son's medicine when I picked it up at the pharmacy. It was early afternoon, and I was between multiple appointments and listening to a CE, so I figured I could multitask. However, due to traffic delays, I was running behind and did not follow my SOP (Standard Operating Procedure) with this task.

Have you cut corners? Not cleaning up something the way you should have and had to redo it then, or couldn't find the tool because you didn't put it back and, as such, lost more time than you saved?

Did you jump through an application wicked quick to try and hit a deadline and realize you missed a signature? You now have to go back and get it so that you don't miss the cutoff that pushed you to go too fast.

Moved too fast in the kitchen and spilled what you were preparing so that all the other effort leading up to that point was wasted?

Pilots have pre-flight checklists for one reason: to ensure nothing gets missed and minimize the potential of something bad happening because a small detail is overlooked. Surgeons do this too. Granted, the downside potential is much greater for them, but their ingrained habit of sticking to the process allows a much higher level of safety that we all count on. Do you have processes in place to minimize the downside with each client? To maximize your potential on the upside?

We use feeder lists and agendas with every client as part of our SOPs to ensure we don't skip anything important, even after 10,000+ meetings. The feeder lists make it easy for the client to help us help other people within their sphere of influence, and having them every time ensures we get paid consistently instead of winging it and hoping to make revenue. We don't NEED them until the time that we forget because people are harried, and time (and tempers) are short. And in that moment of crisis, we need it and are glad to have it in hand, that fallback written bit of training.

"In case of emergency, keep calm and follow procedures."

So that 30 seconds I didn't take to verify the medicine, assuming it was the filled as written versus the generic that doesn't interact with my kid well and is essentially useless, allowing his ADHD to run wild like a crazed squirrel? Yeah, you guessed it. I go back to get it replaced with the good stuff (a twenty-minute drive each way for the 30 seconds I saved) and they won't do it; now I have to call the insurance company and the doctor, invest probably another few hours to get this rectified and deal with the chaos for probably two weeks.

That thirty seconds was totally worth ignoring my procedure.

Slice the Gordian Knot

I have a coaching client who is like myself in many ways: he grew up having to work for what he wanted, played competitive sports to learn lessons and as an outlet, and has built an extremely successful business by applying the mindsets and lessons from these two areas. And like many of us who have built successful businesses, he spoils his spouse and kids. They have never known the hunger that drives this guy, and they never will because, as a good spouse and parent, he has ensured they want nothing, with its advantages and disadvantages. (As an aside, check out "David and Goliath" by Malcolm Gladwell, which discusses how disadvantages such as growing up poor or dyslexia can become incredible advantages such as *"desirable difficulties"*).

T (as we will call him) was complaining because, once again, someone had used up the toilet paper and not replaced the roll. There is no cabinet in that bathroom, so there is no place to hide a backup (like I do because my hooligans always forget, hence this writing). His spouse doesn't want a little rack in the room as it would mess up the aesthetics (again something T and I agree on as a "who cares what the thing looks like, does it work?" blue collar kid attitude). An impasse, with a dependency on flawed human beings, to remember to take an action (check before going to the bathroom, in a moment of panic potentially, to ensure you have what you need at the last second) under emotional duress and time constraints. At best, it is a highly flawed and inconsistent patch job solution that reflects how too many people in our industry operate in their everyday business: last-second chaos and confusion instead of a plan and smooth operations because of preplanning and process. The process ensures superior results.

And then, while listening to some Iron Maiden on my run (long songs and historical stories, great for cranking out endurance workouts), I had a eureka moment: slice the Gordian Knot. For those unfamiliar with the tale, the Phrygians lacked a king in Ancient Greece, and the Oracle declared the next man driving an ox cart into the city would rule. A hard-working peasant farmer named Gordia did so and became king. His son tied the cart to a post with vines and dedicated it to Zeus. Over the years, the vines grew impossibly intricate, and the Oracle declared that whoever could undo the knot would rule the lands after Gordia (hence the Gordian Knot). Centuries passed, Phrygia fell into disarray and became a vassal state of the Persian Empire. In his early days of conquest, Alexander the Great knew of the prophecy and came to Phrygia. Gazing upon the Knot with a fire and desire that would take him all the way to India in his conquest, he contemplated this barrier, this lock sealing the treasure of Asia. Drawing his sword with one mighty swing, Alexander cleft the Knot in half, a non-linear resolution to the problem. He then conquered most of the known world, spreading Hellenic culture and securing his place in history.

Old problems require new thinking to be resolved, or else like the Gordian Knot, they will keep you out of the promised land of success.

In the twenty-third century, there was a test all who wished to be a Captain had to undergo. A test of will and resolve in the face of impossible odds. It was a test designed to fail everyone so that they would have to face their own death and that of all their shipmates to fail and grow from it. I talk, of course, about the Kobayashi Maru, the Star Trek leadership test where all command cadets lose their ship and must face the reality of failure and death and the burden of command. It was foolproof, designed to be unwinnable.

Until James T Kirk beat it.

He changed the rules to beat the unbeatable.

He looked at the unsolvable problem in a different way and found a solution.

Mathematics teaches us that problems can have only three potential outputs: no solution, a single, unique answer, or an infinite number of correct answers. As an optimist, I refuse the first as it represents a nihilistic attitude towards real-world issues. We need to look with more than our eyes and think in a higher dimension to alter the outcome and innovate an answer. And my rebellious streak pushes me towards the last, the infinite solution set, because we can always take a different path to the destination. This is what education is about finding new ideas and ways to solve problems. It is what Kirk will do (in the 23rd Century), what I do, and what Alexander did. Think differently than you have in the past if you want different results in the future, to paraphrase Einstein.

So, T? He needs to get a bidet and never has to worry about toilet paper. A better solution to a crappy situation.

Think differently. Think non-linearly and non-traditionally. Cut the Gordian Knot, and conquer your world.

SKILL SET

Play Ball

Summer means baseball, and I spent some time at my 16-year-old nephew's games this weekend. This young man had some excellent insights:

1. *"I try to get on base 1-2 times per game."* You don't have to get a hit every time up if you have enough plate appearances. And a walk still gets you on base and potentially allows your team to score.
2. *"If it's outside my comfort zone, I just let it go."* If the ball is outside, don't swing. Don't strike yourself out. Not everyone is a good client, so let those who aren't just pass you by.
3. *"I kept an eye on the ball all the way in."* If you take your eye off the ball at the last second, even if you have done everything right up to that point, you'll still ground out.
4. *"I watched where the other players were and that they bobbled it."* Yeah, other people's mistakes can create an opportunity for you to advance or score.
5. "I ran hard right out of the box." Don't wait until partway through the year (or play) to start running hard. From the instant of contact, bust it!
6. *"I listened to my coach and did as they said."*
7. *"I practiced that."*

This young man might not make it to the Big Leagues, but he's already got a championship attitude that will serve him well on the diamond and in the office. Maybe you should consider his insights and then play ball!

May I Ask You a Question?

"Let me ask you a question." Such a powerful and underutilized phrase, the master key of unlocking the human psyche and profitable relationships.

Do you doubt it? Remember the last time someone in a relaxed environment asked you if They could ask you a question. How did you feel? Proud? Curious? In charge?

And what did you do? You answered and probably opened up a bit and talked. You discussed and revealed things about yourself that you weren't intending to share before that conversation.

Even if the other person did not use a Socratic dialogue to lead you to specific conclusions that they desired or to have you reveal particular information, the fact that they asked you questions and you answered created a transfer of power from you to them even though you perceived that you were in command because you were doing most of the talking.

The old adage "he who asks the questions wields the power" is true in acquisitions, sales discussions, teaching, and therapy scenarios. In fact, multiple clients would proclaim after my sales discussions, "I didn't realize I was going to a therapy session. But thank you. This was unlike anything I thought it would be like."

Questioning, as opposed to calculating, uses older evolutionary parts of the brain and, as such, has a more visceral feel because of the cocktail of neurochemicals released and anyone who has made up their mind or drawn their own conclusions on a subject after self-reflection and questioning understands how powerful the outcome of questions can be. If questions are so powerful in decision-making, why don't we use them more when working with our clients?

Ask more questions. Be curious.

I Object

Object: verb

> a. To offer a reason or argument in opposition.
>
> b. To express or feel disapproval, dislike, or distaste; be averse.

- Taken from dictionary.com

We have all been there. You are discussing with a potential (or actual) client, and you get to the point where you want to be paid for the time you have invested in them, brainstorming for Introductions. And **BANG!** The STOP sign goes up, and this person that you have helped, who was engaged and interacting, suddenly slams the brakes on the forward motion by throwing out, "Well, I don't feel comfortable referring people," or some such clichéd excuse.

Instead of swerving uncontrollably and crashing, you must alter the situation and retake control of the discussion and relationship. But you need not panic. Remember your training and practice to maintain your progress and get through the potential accident. If you can remain calm and remove the fear from yourself and your client, you will continue on the journey together and build your Introduction-Based Business.

Previously, we addressed WHY you need to practice achieving mastery of your language and HOW to practice. Now, let us focus on WHAT to practice: being nonplussed when the client throws an objection at you.

First and foremost, review the discussions on Upfront Contracting, the deal before the deal where you get the client to agree that if you create value, then you earn the right to Introduce it. This morally binding contract with the client will give you additional leverage that you can use to force them into cognitive dissonance, and the only way out of the uncomfortable position is for them to do the right thing and introduce you to other high-quality people. Failing to establish this agreement before entering into your process with the potential client removes you from the moral high ground and weakens your position.

Assuming that you have properly laid the groundwork with your process and have actually brought value to your client in the discussion, handling the objections is a simple matter of Acknowledging, Addressing, Redirecting, Requesting, and Repeating. Most objections become as ephemeral as the morning mist by creating an internal mental process of Acknowledging, Addressing, Redirecting, Requesting, and Repeating (AARRR, as a pirate would say).

Acknowledging: The worst thing you can do is ignore what a client says. They are expressing a feeling, an emotion, a concern that often originates in the older parts of the brain. They are telling you that they are afraid. Failure to acknowledge their concern will make you seem like a manipulator as you will use neo-cortical reasoning to overcome crocodile brain "fight or flight" reactions. The computer logic of modern human thinking will always lose to the million-year-old gut response. So, you should literally say, "I hear what you are saying. In other words, you feel like..." and reframe their objection. This shows them on a fundamental level that you "get" them and why they are worried about introducing you to others.

By embracing the fear and then moving it slowly toward a rational exploration thereof, removes the power of the fear and slows the situation from panic mode. If you ignore this step, you remain in danger.

Addressing: Now that the client's croc brain has been stroked sufficiently that they are no longer ready to run away, we need to interact with the middle part of the brain that focuses on social interactions and emotions, our monkey brain as it were. This is where you calmly and slowly discuss the emotional why of their objection. Remind them of their moral contract with you, and invoke the name of the person who introduced you so that you can capture part of the sheep mentality effect (everyone else gives introductions, don't you want to be part of the cool kid crowd?) and actually answer the objection (how will you contact the person, few people mind being contacted because 75%+ of Americans have expressed desire for the products you provide, explain your process again, etc.) and then get them to once again agree that you are a professional that adds value and wouldn't do anything untoward to ruin your reputation or relationship with referrer.

Redirecting: moving their attention away from whatever the now-addressed issue is critical. Transition their focus off of the past (with its negative emotions or connotations) and onto the present and future. Guide them, lead them. This is what clients want: to be shown that their fears can be left behind and they can move to a better position. Transitioning into a newer state of lower anxiety is a critical skill in all sales situations.

THEN **Request:** Ask again, going straight into a soft demand for Introductions with a phrase such as "so based upon this, who do you know that both you and (referrer's name) know that should get a chance to meet me so I can take them through a helpful discussion like we've had today?" Ask, and you shall receive. Roll straight into a triangulated Introduction that draws upon the strength of the positive emotions you have engendered with the person you are sitting with and the halo effect of the relationship of the person who got you into that meeting to get that first, hardest Introduction from this potential client. Once you get a single Introduction it is easy to brainstorm on additional people.

Repeat: keep going through the cycle as often as needed to assuage their fears and remove all objections. Smile and turn it into a game because even if they are being a bit of a jerk and trying to exert a power dynamic on you, after the fourth or fifth objection they will respect you for sticking to your guns and laugh. And you'll get your introductions. Too many Advisors miss out because they handle one objection or two but aren't ready and willing to overcome five or seven or as many as it takes to get paid.

After a few iterations, if the person you are talking with is an ethical individual and you address their fears and emotions and leverage the social aspects of the how the mind works, you will be paid for your time and your journey will continue.

Remember that objections come from averse feelings, based upon their experiences and cultural biases and heuristics from popular opinion. Acknowledge how they feel and why, gently but firmly show why that feeling or bias does not apply in your situation and prod them along to open up their mind and their Rolodex. Be calm, be controlled, and objections are little more than bumps on the road of your journey to build an Introduction Based Business.

Win the Morning 2

Hey there, sleepy head.

Wakey wakey, time to get up. C'mon, rise and shine.

Get up and get moving. Get up and get going.

Enough. Get your ass out of bed!

Jocko Willink, Navy SEAL leader, proclaims, *"Win the morning. Win the day."* How do you win the morning?

First, go to bed! Get to sleep earlier than you think is cool. This will allow you to be rested, to fight and win.

Secondly, get up early—dark o'clock—and watch the sun come up, filling the world with hope. Sunrise is coffee for the soul, and you can start dominating while others are still dreaming.

Third, get your blood pumping. Exercise early so your body is kicked into overdrive in the morning and your metabolism revives all day. Repeatedly doing this will make your body stronger and give you the endurance to compete all day while others peter out because they are physically weak.

Simultaneous to this, feed your mind and soul. Listening to YouTube motivational or educational videos while you do your planks, miles, or lifts will strengthen your resolve, get your mind ready for the day, and strengthen your spirit so that you don't flag in the face of adversity. Some of my favorites are **MULLIGAN BROTHERS RED FROST MOTIVATION FAR FROM AVERAGE THE HUMAN KAIZEN**

EXPERT Now fuel your body. Healthy food, not a gut-busting grease bomb or chemical concoction. Protein will help your mind and keep you full: failure to fuel means you will bonk before lunch and lose the day.

Now get your butt to work.

One More

What is the value of one more?

In economics, we know that there is the idea of diminishing marginal returns, which says that adding more of anything (money, workers, Legos) creates an increase in a desired output (widget production or happiness) but less than the increase in output from the last addition. Think about it: that first drink after a long workweek is awesome: the moment it hits your lips, the mental sigh is almost audible. And the second sip is practically as good. Yet the third drink brings much less joy than that initial one. You have reached diminishing marginal returns after that first drink.

Now we can contrast this with sub-critical level increases. If you earn $1,000,000 a year, an extra $50 is essentially nothing to you, yet for most struggling new sales Representatives, an extra fifty bucks could be the difference between filling their gas tank to get to an appointment and making that critical sale or not. More is not just more; it could mean the difference between failure and success, a binary output. This could be considered a "quantum return," where a tiny increase in input creates a completely different and superior overall output.

In the middle ground between these extremes, we have a fairly linear world where we can predict increases in output based on input. You have probably had a sales manager talk about your ratios and increasing your activity so that you can sell more products, thus increasing your output and hitting your (and their) goals. This is the realm we will focus on for this discussion.

Going back to that $50 number referenced above, that number (per a few different career companies in the insurance world) is the approximate value of an introduction for a relatively new financial Representative, so it makes a good starting point for discussion.

One additional monthly introduction (or referral or prospect, as many managers still call them) is $600 a year. This is de minimis and statistically insignificant to cashflow and survival statistics (long-range remaining in the profession as opposed to leaving the industry).

One additional weekly introduction is 52 x $50 or $2,600 annually. This is enough to keep those on the margins around, and the trailing production it generates through renewals, additional sales, and additional future introductions could be worth about 10x that. This should be enough to grab a newer Representative's attention. Getting a single additional introduction a week is literally asking one more person a week **"If we switched seats and you were the Financial Advisor, who is the first person you would call?"** You should try it; it works.

But if you asked that one question every day, just once, and got one additional introduction a day? That is worth over $10,000 to you this year. $100k+ over time, probably much more due to compounding issues. It's a big deal.

But this year?

Ten thousand dollars.

To ask one question once a day.

THAT is the power of one more.

The Trichotomy of Control

In "A Guide to the Good Life {the ancient art of stoic joy}" William Irvine expands Epictetus' Dichotomy of Control into a third area in a manner that every professional should harken to, as it is a superior model for how we interact with the world, and clients in particular.

The Dichotomy of Control is echoed in the Serenity Prayer:

> "God, grant me the Serenity to accept the things I cannot change, The Courage to change the things I can, And the Wisdom to know the difference."

What we can change, we should strive vigorously to improve; what we cannot change, we must placidly ignore, and the most difficult part is separating the chaos of the world into the two camps. For anyone who is driven by a passion to impact the world, hit goals, or love for another, admitting we cannot control some things is anathema to us. We will literally beat our head against a wall to try and do something, anything, to change these things, whether it is a failed deal or a bad medical diagnosis or a failed relationship.

Being powerless is the greatest fear of the powerful.

The Dichotomy of Control states that there are things within our power and things that are beyond our power. The things within our power are purely internal: our thoughts, our emotions, our decisions. Anything beyond our minds is outside our power: we cannot control getting sick, the weather, taxes, or the bad decisions of others.

This is where Irvine expands to a third area: things under our **influence**. Using the example of a tennis match, he says we can control how much we practice and serve, but the moment the opponent returns the serve, we are in the third realm of influence. We can somewhat but not entirely control our foot movement and our swing, but we are reacting to an external stimulus (the ball) and have incomplete control over what happens with our body placement, ball contact, and the ball's flight. Our influence is limited but not zero, which applies to everything from volleying the tennis ball to our drive to work to discussions with clients.

So, let's apply the trichotomy of control when interacting with a client. Things we can completely control are our preparation, our mindset when we begin, and the words we say. We have no control over technical glitches in Zoom (but we can have a backup plan, as modern stoic Jocko Willink would point out), over what the competition has presented, or if the client is having a bad day because of getting caught in traffic or their kid acting up in the middle of the night. We can influence everything else by listening and observing (gathering as much info as possible), the rapidity of speaking, and our physical reactions to the situation. Once in the meeting, this is by far the largest segment of the interaction: influential but uncontrollable. We must strive to do our best in this space, as it is where our growth lies.

Internalizing our goals for the meeting to something we can control (such as "I will ask for Introductions") is better than depending on an outcome we cannot control ("I am walking out of here with the business, no matter what"), which is an external validation of our efforts and fleeting in terms of the rewards. Focusing on our actions (both their quality and quantity) is measurable, semi-predictable, and under our control, instead of hanging our happiness on another choice. This is equally applicable in business or personal situations. Knowing you did everything right is more rewarding than any individual lucky break because the pattern of success comes from within as opposed to from without. It can and will hurt in the moment of loss, but the internal acceptance of doing your best with the situation allows the pain to fade more quickly than if you are hung up on outcome-oriented happiness driven by others.

Developing the wisdom to know what is under your influence versus out of your control takes experience, discovering that you didn't get the result you wanted to not because of somebody two hundred miles away but because you didn't listen enough or ask the right questions or couldn't control your actions. Failures should be learning opportunities. Learning to do the best you can where you can and not waste energy on external things beyond your reach is maturity developing as a professional and a person. You might not become a Marcus Aurelius, but you will be a better version of yourself, and that is something totally within your control.

Mutation

A mutation is a tiny change that, if it improves the species, is passed on to the next generation, eventually becoming prevalent and pushing out the outmoded ability, standard, or technology. Evolution in animals takes hundreds of generations to spread, so ten thousand years for humans and under a year for fruit flies. In tech, it takes a few years to completely outmode the old and replace it with the better, faster, more resilient, and powerful.

You, as a human, though, can evolve your business daily. No, you won't have the healing power of Wolverine, but every day, you can break your old you, improve, and overnight, heal from the previous day's wounds and be better. This was the Norse idea of Heaven for the brave, Valhalla, where the warriors of worth would fight and die every day, then rise up, heal, feast, and fight the next day better than before. We should adopt this evolutionary improvement approach to our businesses.

Choose one aspect of your business that will directly impact your output. It could be your attitude, close skills, or questions you ask in initial client meetings. Let's focus on Introductions, as that is ultimately the primary driver of all other components of your Introduction-Based Business.

Suppose you honestly assess your ability to continuously gather high-quality introductions to the individuals or organizations that you need to grow your business. In that case, you will probably agree that you have tremendous room for growth. You could get a lot better, and it won't take a Herculean effort to start the improvement process on a very short cycle. You could probably do something tiny today to get better tomorrow, such as:

Running a list of potential names to feed your clients this week.

Memorizing a new IQ (Introduction Question), such as "Who is the most driven person you know?" so that it easily slips off your tongue like an actor repeating a line they have rehearsed for years.

Write out your introduction language.

Practice your responses to commonly asked questions from clients so that your responses are as ingrained as a Viking warrior's battle responses.

Having everything you need to call new potential clients prepped so you can grab your joe, sit down, and go.

Assume you chose to improve a process like having your phoning prepped. Day 1 should be easy to show improvement. Day 2 is a little harder because the easiest gains were made just by starting. Day 3 is a little more difficult as you have captured some of the easier issues. Keep at it, though, for an entire week because the incremental gains on that last day are the most important.

Next week, choose something different to work on WHILE MAINTAINING the old discipline/ improvement. Select a skill for this week, like practicing handling objections every day for five minutes in the morning. By the end of this week, that particular skill will be substantially improved.

Keep rotating between processes and skills you can practice. Even if some of the old skills lose a bit of their edge, the net effect is constant improvement in critical areas for you to build and run your Introduction-Based Business. This is exactly the process that Benjamin Franklin used to improve himself across 13 areas he identified as needing improvement to become a better businessman and leader. It obviously works if you apply the idea.

What will you notice in a month? Situations that would break you no longer scare you because you have practiced them a hundred times, so you no longer fear the unknown but rather welcome the challenge of an objection. Your mornings are more efficient because you habitually prepare for your day and sit down, ready to perform. The daily growth positively impacts your attitude, making you more effective in multiple areas of your daily activities. Your confidence is better than before, and you can start seeing it reflected in your production.

Now keep switching your daily improvement focus for a quarter, sometimes cycling back to previous skills. After one day of practice, they are as sharp as ever; after three, they are better than ever, and at the end of that week, they are beyond where you previously thought possible. Your processes are humming like a well-tuned machine, and your paychecks are consistently good to great.

Most importantly, at this point, you have meta-awareness of your business. Not only do you understand it deeply, almost intuitively, but you are able to start thinking about all its aspects and the whole on a much different level. You have an attitude of growth, a mindset of possibilities and excellence, and a desire to improve and excel. Evolution is now in your DNA.

So, take that first little step. Make that tiny incremental change. Start on that journey to excellence. Some days, it will be tough, and you'll get mentally bruised, but you'll heal and fight again the next day stronger and better. And better. And better. They won't make comic books or movies about you or put your face on the $100 bill, but your evolution could become the stuff of legend.

Continuous Improvement

This weekend, I earned another Instructor Certificate in a completely different field of endeavor. I am trying to continuously better myself to help others grow and develop. And the most informative parts of the weekend did not come from a book.

Once you have a good handle on things, the highest level of learning is from doing and discussing.

Doing is obvious. Any skill, from asking for Introductions to cooking to firing a weapon, is enhanced by committed practice. Generally, the first hundred repetitions are learning the skill, and the next 10,000 are mastering it.

But when you are in that few hundred-plus range of reps, pausing and talking with others doing the same thing is invaluable. especially if they have more varied experience than you because you hear a different perspective on the technique or issue. A new set of eyes can let you see a different facet of the diamond.

Attend conferences.

Go to training sessions sponsored by providers.

Join your professional organization.

Create a study group.

Force yourself to look at your business from an external point of view, to see the components in a different light. Look through another's eyes at yourself, what you are doing, and why.

This is one way to accelerate your growth as a person and professional.

Commit to continuous improvement, and your business and life will know no bounds.

If you are not yet a <u>NAIFA member</u>, you should consider joining and improving yourself with your peers.

Learning from others on a similar journey but slightly different paths will supplement your learning and doing in unexpected and financially rewarding ways.

Balance Daniel-San

"Balance, Daniel-san! Must have balance!"- The Karate Kid
You read that in Mr. Miyagi's voice, and that's good. That lesson is eternal, the most enduring part of Pat Morita's legacy.

And by balance, I don't mean a donut in each hand, although that technically is a well-balanced meal if you alternate which one you bite.

The Ying Yang symbol represents the ever-changing dichotomy of nature: order and chaos, masculine and feminine, creation and destruction. Whenever one dominates over the other for too long, everything moves out of balance, and the universe attempts to correct the situation, a dynamic system that tends towards a means.

Many of us have crushing responsibilities: businesses, families, and others depending upon us. We do what we must in stressful situations that seem to come wave after wave. That's called life. But like Daniel kicking the waves as he trained, there needs to be an ebb and flow that we adjust to so we don't drown.

Here are several techniques I have adopted to help balance my fifteen-hour days so I don't burn out. Some of them might help.

1. Set an alarm on your phone for midmorning and midafternoon. When it goes off, set a one-minute timer, close your eyes, and breathe slower and deeper.

2. Eat your veggies. Seriously.
3. Create a morning routine that includes:
   a. Saying thank you for another day
   b. Thinking about those people you really love
   c. Read something to nourish your mind and spirit. "Every Day Excellence" is a good one; I'm just saying.
   d. Spend a few minutes awakening your body. Stretch, walk, calisthenics, whatever works for you.
   e. Don't skip breakfast!
4. Smile at people whenever you can.
5. Schedule a date a week. It could be with your partner; it could be with yourself.
6. Read something (not directly work-related) for 15 minutes daily. I use audiobooks to take advantage of windshield time in the car.
7. Talk to (or at least message) a friend daily. Maybe send them something funny, because this will help both of you. Laughter is one of the best stress reducers known.
8. Take a walk. Every hour or so, stand up and walk for a few minutes to stretch your legs, get the blood flowing, and reset your eyesight. There are times when we need to push ourselves very hard and times when we need to rest so our mind and body can recover. The seasons have a rhythm, be it the natural ones outside or the work environment. Pay attention to the signs to see if you are getting out of balance.

SKILL SET

During the tournament, when the prize was in sight, Daniel suffered a horrible injury. He came to grips with it, understanding the need for balance with his quest, his relationship, and, most importantly, himself. We have all faced the devastating injury, even if not physical. The question is, do we learn to have balance with ourselves and heal?

Seduction

"My clients all love me because I'm easy to love."

Horsefeathers. Client relationships are very similar to dating, and we won't talk about the intimacy components but merely focus on the relational dynamics that are similar in both situations.

In the initial stages of a relationship, be it romantic or business based, people are putting on their best behavior and trying their darndest to get the other person to like them. It is not necessarily Laing's false Self-psychotic interactions, but it is more like a covering of our flaws and enhancing our better components while giving extra weight to what the other person is representing, a bias towards their not truly reflected preferences. We see the best, most interesting parts of the other person and do our best to interact with what they present, subtly altering our own actions in a dance of illusions.

This is the Seduction stage, where both sides are trying to get something without necessarily being authentic and can't be true to the other due to the duality of misrepresentation. Both are lying to the other and themselves at various levels. It is rare (and requires great emotional integrity and personal awareness) to resist "giving in" on all the little things in the initial interactions to prevent compounding falsehoods that repeatedly destroy nascent partnerships because of an over-eagerness to please and be pleased. Saying "No" to a seemingly good thing is difficult, especially if the current situation is not good and there is any form of desperation or unmet need. Experience is one of the critical factors in seeing through the other's illusion and preventing us from playing the same game of fantasy and delusion.

If this relationship proceeds, there must be a discovery of the truths and acceptance that neither was sincere in the initial stages of flirting (professionally or amorously). Now, suppose the entire idea is a one-time transaction/fling. In that case, Seduction might meet the short-term needs of both sides, but to have a lasting situation that leads to growth and sustainability, a more fundamental and factual foundation must be built. Sometimes, a partnership can move into the next stage even without the proper groundwork, but as with a building, holes in the support structure will inevitably lead to catastrophic failure.

The next stage is where we see the "All my clients love me," "I'm easy to love," or "I can't believe how perfect they are." Anyone married knows the Honeymoon stage: all is good, flaws don't exist (or are cute instead of annoying and red flags). Early in the client development process, we see this, the potential but not the problems that will become headaches and eventually nightmares if not addressed. The "oh, she's just a little restrained" is actually "she's emotionally devoid and covering", or "he's just a big kid all the time," covering his lack of development and assuming the responsibilities of adulthood that can sabotage the relationship. As we say in ethics: "just" is a dangerous word because it is a slippery slope to cross lines that should not be crossed. Suppose you haven't been in many relationships (professional and personal). In that case, the Honeymoon covers the issues with makeup that can hide the hideousness that we would never accept over time. Many divorces (business and marital) occur because these traits are uncovered and worsen over time if unaddressed. Honeymoon periods vary, but interpersonal relationships tend to be over in six months or so when the stark reality of life messes with the fairy tale. In professional relationships, it depends upon the cycle of the business and the number of interactions, so anywhere from a few months to a few years before the love that was there early is forced to confront the difficulties of actual actions and tough choices. If you have a habit of jettisoning partners (or clients) when it starts getting intense, it could reflect the flaws in the relationship from the outset and a signal that you should re-evaluate how you present yourself during the Seduction stage of opening interactions.

Suppose the couple (business or erotic partners, even merely intense friendships with no physical component) can get through the Honeymoon phase and start showing resiliency and adaptability. In that case, they can address the flaws and have the difficult conversations around the misrepresentations presented early that the dynamic is built off of, there is a possibility of them building honest communication. Returning to Laing, they have stripped away the False Selves and are interacting on more of a True Self to True Self basis, even if it is not as pretty or exciting. It is real and more powerful, lasting but potentially explosive like a semi-permanent nuclear fusion instead of a chemical reaction in the outer electron levels that can easily be reversed via outside influences.

These sorts of highly intense communications and relationships (think Twin Flames if spiritual is your realm instead of nuclear physics or interpersonal dynamics) are NOT easy; they are volatile and require an immense and ongoing effort but are true, powerful, and can last a lifetime if both parties are willing to admit their flaws, their issues, and look to themselves and the partner for the last pieces of their fulfillment in a well-grounded assessment of both themselves and the other without neediness or fear.

True friends tell each other what they need to hear, not what they want. This is for lovers, business partners, and providers. The ability to have early difficult conversations, to not chase because you know what your own limits are and are comfortable waiting for the right one (person or client) instead of going for "good enough" and repeating the mistakes of the past based upon experience and confidence in your own value (even if others can't yet see it) is the strong bedrock that long term relationships are built off of. It might not be as exciting or sexy as the game of Seduction, it might not be as intoxicating as the fantasy of the Honeymoon, but it is deeper and stronger and can last decades by being real. And that is the greatest relationship of them all.

Tough Love

Ok, time for some tough love.

You are not living up to your potential.

Admit it. Look at your calendar and then look in the mirror.

How many days did you spend, eight hours face-to-face with clients last week? I bet you the answer is "zero." Isn't that ultimately what you are paid to do? How many hours last week were you in this situation of directly interacting with the people who could give you money?

What are you doing with your time?

Let's expand our definition of productive work to include other activities directly related to delivering your services, such as phoning for appointments, following up with clients/potential clients, analyzing stuff for clients, etc. Did you do this for a solid eight hours any day last week?

Didn't think so.

"But I'm sooo busy".

BS.

You are wasting a tremendous amount of time.

Do you get paid to drive to a client's site? Probably not. Wasted time.

Cold calling? (eye roll)

Dorking around on the internet?

Between 8 a.m. and 4 p.m., you should only do client-facing activities or things that lead directly to client-facing activities (like picking up the phone to schedule appointments).

No getting your dry cleaning. Don't go to the gym.

Work.

See the people.

Ask for introductions.

Do your job.

Or else you are going to have to get a real job because you failed out for not working hard enough.

So enough tough love inspiration. Get to work.

Now!

Psychology of Capitalism

Let's discuss the psychology of capitalism as it relates to introductions. I spent a few minutes on it in my presentation "Becoming an Introduction Machine" and in the book with Dr. Stolk, "Choices: Creating a Financial Services Career," but given the recent failures of faith and action of some Reps I worked with, I believe we need an in-depth discussion on the subject.

First off, a definition.

Capitalism (noun): an economic system in which investment in and ownership of the means of production, distribution, and exchange of wealth is made and maintained chiefly by private individuals or corporations, especially as contrasted to cooperatively or state-owned means of wealth.

This is from dictionary.com and is a good technical, broad definition, but I have a working one that I like because we can break down the components further. My personal operational definition of capitalism is "A system of free exchange of items or services of value for profit." Let's break this down into the building blocks.

System: an interacting group of components that function to create outputs.

Free exchange: interactions are chosen by the participants instead of being forced to work together through government or other mandates. NB: a client can choose not to work with you, but you can choose not to accept or even fire a bad client. Never forget this.

Items or services: physical goods or intangible items such as intellectual property-based upon knowledge, experience, and insight.

Of value: useful and/or holding pecuniary worth.

For-profit is a situation in which all parties to the transaction feel they got at least what they needed.

I want to explore these last two pieces (of value for profit) because this is the crux of the issue regarding financial advisors asking for introductions.

Value differs from the price paid because of the individual interpretation of value. Paying an attorney $240 an hour for 5 hours equates to a price-paid tag of $1,200, but if that is what the dollar cost was to establish a scholarship fund in the name of your parents, it is fairly obvious that the value exceeds the price paid. We have all paid $5 or $50 for something and then said, "That was a waste of money", and we have spent nothing for a walk in the park with someone we loved, and that memory is cherished and valued immensely. Do not confuse the exchange of dollars for the value of something: preventing a client from making a half-million-dollar mistake is worth over half a million bucks to them, whether they pay $10,000 or even no dollars.

Value is in the mind and heart more than the wallet.

As to "for profit", this concept derives from value but extends it in that we need to consider additional economic and psychological factors. One consideration is the economic value received, and what was exchanged for it. An economic value received of a few hundred dollars for an hour of time sacrificed is generally profitable, especially if what is gained will continue to generate benefits. This could be skills acquired, compounding interest, tax breaks that carry forward, or productivity hacks. Anything that keeps producing value with little or no additional investment is highly profitable.

Another dimension of profit is the psychological avoidance of failure. Knowing that you have a plan in place for the prevention of a data breach and the nightmare that could ensue, or that your kid's college is all set as long as you stay on course, or that you will run your first marathon as long as you stick with the training program and don't get injured are of great value. Removing doubt is an important service. Insurance is the financial removal of doubt via contract. Removing mental doubts should be compensated appropriately, too.

What is being able to sleep at night worth?

In many instances, avoiding a loss can be financially modeled as to its value, but we all make gut-check assessments on this parameter. As a financial advisor, you create tremendous profit for clients every single day, helping them avoid losses of six and seven figures with your guidance, even if they don't buy a product from you. A CPA or LLM will charge them hundreds an hour for that, and the client will pay these professionals without blinking an eye because they know the value of the losses avoided and calculate the profit in relation to the cost and how much peace of mind, they derive from knowing that they are "all set". They should be valuing your time, similarly, as should you.

A further aspect of "profitable" is the desire to do business again in the future, as there are emotional, relational, and other benefits beyond monetary around the relationship itself. Trust is a component of this, as is respect. If your client likes and respects you and believes that you acted in their best long-range interests instead of trying to maximize your short-term cash flow via a transaction, they will see advantage and profit in working with you over time. We all know that acquiring a new client is difficult, time-consuming, and costly regardless of the industry. It is also difficult for the client from an emotional investment perspective, so ensuring that you are doing the right things to ensure future work with them is critical to creating a profitable relationship for all involved.

Now that we have broken down, explored, and rebuilt the idea of Capitalism, we can analyze mentally embracing its value for your business. Financial services are the easiest place to make a quarter of a million dollars a year and the hardest place to make $50k a year. But believing in the free exchange of value for profit will get you to that quarter million and beyond because the only limiting factor for an insurance and investment professional like yourself is the limitations you are self-imposing by not being paid properly for your time via introductions.

"But I didn't sell them anything."

"I'll wait until the time is right."

"We ran out of time."

"It didn't feel right asking."

All BS excuses because you don't believe in your core that you added value to this person in that meeting and deserve compensation. YOU are imposing a limit on your earnings because of doubt.

Did you bring them value in that meeting?

Take out a piece of paper. Now. Right now. Stop reading this and grab a piece of paper so you can write 10 ways you bring value to a potential client in an initial meeting. Some examples:

1. Did you suggest they update their beneficiary designations? You potentially saved their heirs dozens of hours and thousands of dollars.
2. Get basic legal paperwork in order or updated. Immense psychological relief and many hours of legal fees avoided if anything happens.
3. Contribute more to their employer-sponsored plan to get more matches. That is FREE money you now have going into their future.
4. Recommend they take advantage of an employer-sponsored benefit. They are getting
5. Don't you deserve to receive additional coverage or value for this?
6. Initiate a discussion of savings philosophy between spouses they have never had. You might have just headed off a divorce, as monetary miscommunication is one of the leading factors in marriages ending. How much did you just save them?!

These are five very high-value examples; with ten minutes, you can easily come up with a dozen more. Keep this list you create and refer to it, as it is your creation and, as such, more valuable to you convincing yourself than my external ideas. And remember this concept of self-selling, as it is useful for clients, as their rationale is more powerful than anything you can tell them.

How much value are you creating for that potential client in an initial meeting?

$10,000?

$25,000?

More?

Aren't five figures of value from you to them worth something?

You DESERVE and EARN five introductions for what you have done. You just need to get that person you are sitting with to acknowledge this by literally asking, "Was this time well invested? Did I create value for our time together? What was the most valuable to you?"

Then shut your mouth and let them tell you what a good job you have already done for them in that first meeting. This is incredibly psychologically important because it is their words, their voice, them convincing themselves how much value they have derived. You can comment and guide them slightly, but most of these few minutes need to be them expressing your impact on them.

Then ASK! It doesn't matter if you feed them back names from your questionnaire of people they mentioned, feed them categories (like an attorney, boss, godparents to the kids, etc.) or hand them a list of their associates from your research (my favored approach). You can even say, "Whip out your cell; who are the last five people you called?"

Just ASK and make it easy for them to pay you with the names of other high-quality people you should talk to.

If you have done a decent job of helping them so far and believe in yourself and the value you have brought, five introductions should be a non-issue. They could keep going and naming people they want you to call, and a dozen or more is not unusual if you focus on improving your potential client's life with your knowledge and positive mindset.

Understand your impact and the intrinsic value of your guidance and know in your soul that you deserve to be properly compensated for it. We have stripped some of the neurochemical basis out of this discussion, but it all hinges on this: sell yourself on your value, create value for the client, and then collect your payment in introductions.

That is the difference between making $50k and $250k. Embrace your Capitalistic nature and demand fair compensation for the value you bring.

Afterword:

Watch this video by Patrick Bet David, founder of PHP, for a great talk on why Capitalism is important.

I especially love his reason #10: Capitalism forgives. It doesn't matter that you used to not believe you deserved introductions for helping someone in an initial meeting, it matters what you believe and do now. It doesn't matter that in the past you failed to get referrals because you didn't think you deserved them for only pointing out five ways to improve your client's life that had nothing to do with buying a product from you, today you know better and realize you saved them tens of thousands of dollars in taxes and deserve to be paid for it.

The Trials of the Master

There was once a martial arts master of exceeding wisdom and skill. His prowess and insight into leaders' minds were renowned across the land, and the Queen summoned him to train her armies and Generals.

When the Master appeared before the Queen, she decided that this humble little man with wispy white hair and a broad smile could not be the deadly Master of legend. Thus, she ordered that he undergo trials to prove his worth to lead her armies into battle, something that the Master did not desire as he was content to sip his tea and teach his students in the mountains. But out of respect for the Queen, he consented to the trials.

The first trial was by spear. At a distance of a dozen yards, a soldier threw a razor-sharp spear at the Master's chest, which he easily dodged with a smile and a comment on the soldier's throw, suggesting he lean in more to get more strength into it.

The second trial was by arrow. A young soldier stood two dozen paces away and fired an arrow at the Master, who caught the shaft and mid-flight and suggested the soldier calm his breathing as the missile was off target due to the soldier's excitement.

The third trial was by sword. A soldier stepped forward and thrust at the Master, hacking and chopping away. Each blow barely missed him, sometimes nicking his hair or beard but never materially impacting the Master as he chattered away about staying in movement the properties of water as a teacher, and the virtue of practicing until your tools are an extension of your body. The soldier grew tired over ten minutes of swinging the sword and continuously missing his victim, who seemed to know where he would attack before he did and thus easily avoided the blade. Finally, the Master pushed the exhausted youth over, leaving him in the dust.

The Queen was both upset at the ease with which her soldiers failed and impressed with the Master declared that he should instruct her armies and her Generals in his ways.

"Ah, your Majesty, but I have already done so. Your men and your leaders have learned from the Trial by Spear to commit fully, to put their all into what they do at the moment. In the Trial by Arrow, I demonstrated that your people need to be calm, centered, and non-plussed. Professional soldiers and leaders must have confidence and commitment. And in the Trial by Sword, I hope you picked up on the importance of practice, endurance, and the dangers of becoming rigid, of freezing up. These lessons apply to your soldiers and your leaders, my Queen."

And with that statement, the Master took his tea and his leave.

Independence

If you were to go to dictionary.com for the definition of "Independence", you would find the noun with the following:

1. freedom from the control, influence, support, aid, or the like of others.
2. *Archaic.* a competency

Independence Day is one of the most fun holidays on the calendar in the US. It celebrates one of the most traditional American values, dating back before the earliest hardy Europeans settled on these shores. I wish that you develop independence in the truest sense of the word.

I want you to develop competency in your craft so that you will always have work and add value to your clients while improving yourself to have a greater impact. Mastering the skills to acquire new clients will give you independence in that you will be relieved of the mental burdens of fear and scarcity in that you can and will always be able to make your own future by building relationships from scratch. You will know that everything could be taken from you at work. You could overcome that obstacle by rebuilding your Introduction Based Business with your knowledge of your field and how humans work to recreate a better position and career because the skillset and mindset of networking and doing the best you can are engrained so deeply in you that they will always show. A competency that rises to the level of excellence in introductions and your particular craft.

Once you have evolved from novice through apprentice to Master in your skills, you should develop independence along the financial lines. No more buying leads from data miners or depending upon your office superior to throw crumbs your way. No, hoping for call-ins or walk-ins or attending 7:00 networking meetings with other people who are scrounging for business or cold calling until you want to cry. No more hoping for a lucky break but rather planning for and executing to achieve success. Because you know how to do it and believe you can, and you will.

Develop your front-end activity to the point where you have three dozen open and active files at any moment. Too many real estate agents have three or four potential clients they are working with at any one point, and this paucity of potential keeps them skittish and scared because they do not have enough activity to let the law of large numbers take over. They are so dependent upon every single one of their open inventories closing that they lack an abundance mentality and can't look their client in the eye and give them the tough truth that will garner more respect, business, and introductions. An Advisor with two scores or more open and active cases doesn't worry if a particular client doesn't close because they represent 2.5% of their current potential. Even if that client doesn't come through, another one will and will be replaced in the queue within a day. This gives the Active Advisor the freedom to act in ways the inactive one can't or won't, independence from any particular customer, and the ability to look that person in the eye and say, "I don't need you or your business because I and my family are fine without you. But you and your family need to listen to me because without following my recommendation, you are screwed."

Independence lets you alpha up and speak the truth, thus being more powerful and effective.

As Jocko Willink declared in his bestseller *Discipline Equals, Freedom,* Freedom and Independence are twin ideals, and your daily discipline is the price you will pay for financial and business independence. You need to invest time to hone your craft and build your skills. You need to face difficult and stressful situations to make the resolve to have not easy but critical conversations with clients. Every moment, we are tempted by the easy path that buys us a moment of ease but at a future cost, additional hardships later. Do not choose the easy way; it will ultimately be harder and longer.

Fly

Man was not meant to fly.

So, he made a machine to do so.

Women were not meant to run marathons.

Until they did it.

Reps can't get 30 introductions a week consistently.

Except I did, and you can too.

By using machines and tools to help you fly.

By changing your mindset of what is possible.

By altering your expectations.

Humankind uses its minds and tools to change the world around us, whether it is strapping a sharp rock on a stick to fight off bigger, stronger, fiercer animals early on or developing agriculture to grow consistent food. We need to eat, and over the centuries, through the use of technology, we have become increasingly effective at both farming and hunting.

Are you applying this sort of innovation to your practice, though? Or are you relying on outmoded ideas and processes, ignoring technology, relying on brute force, and hoping to get enough introductions to run your business?

Why?

You have a brain. Use it.

Over 250 million Americans want what you have to offer. There are enough fish in the sea; you just need to be smarter about casting your net and believe there are actually fish below the surface where you can't see them. If you need to feed a village (or your office), you must have a plan.

First, you need to make many attempts. It is said, "The Master has failed more times than an amateur has even tried". You need to cast your net often to catch fish. You must ask whenever you are with a client or potential client for introductions. Not asking is leaving your net out of the water.

Improve your effort.

Secondly, you need to make sure your net isn't broken. Fishermen repair their nets after they return to shore to ensure that they are ready to go out again. Are you looking at the language you are using to ensure that it is not broken? Are you taking the time to stitch it back together, stronger than before, to catch the bigger fish?

Improve your tools.

Third, you need to make sure you have a big enough boat. A small dingy you can row on your own can get you only so far from shore. If you invested in more capacity and assembled a crew you can get out beyond the shallows to where the water is blue, and the fish teem. Fear keeps us in the shallows, content to catch small fry instead of risking and going after whales and swarms of larger fish. Fear of failure and contentment with "just enough," these false limitations we impose upon ourselves and our businesses are like the restriction on the four-minute mile.

Improve your belief.

Yes, you are not physically able to swim two miles, dive down three hundred feet, and wrestle a shark. That is why we build the boat, buy or make nets, and use technology to overcome physical limitations once we have overcome our mental limitations.

That is why millions of women run marathons a year: because they have overcome the mental hurdles.

That is why we fly billions of miles a year: because we have improved technology compensating for our physical shortcomings.

That is why you can and will get thirty introductions this week and every week: you have broken through the mental barrier and are using technology to improve your performance.

Because we were not meant to fly.

We were born to soar.

Centers

If you look back across human history, one of civilization's greatest leaps forward was not the computer or the wheel. It was the discovery of farming.

The ability to plan ahead, plant when appropriate, and patiently await results while cultivating the crops created a fundamental shift from the hunter/gatherer mentality. It allowed us to put down roots and form larger groups, which led to writing laws and culture. Eventually, it would lead to government, trade, specialization of crafts, and technological innovation because we could plan on having food instead of hoping for a good hunt.

Unfortunately, many people who enter sales professions (real estate, financial services, coaching, etc.) never evolve past the hunting/gathering stage, stunting their growth or starving out of the business. They did not build an Introduction-Based Business and embrace the planting/nurturing/harvesting cycle, whether out of fear or short-sightedness. To become truly civilized as a professional, you must embrace trade and develop Centers.

Trade centers have always been centers of economics and culture throughout human history. As these locations grew from hundreds of people to millions (like NYC, Shanghai, London, Rome, etc.), the diversification of trades exploded, as did the wealth of the center and its participants. As Adam Smith explored in Wealth of Nations, specialization of skills in population-dense areas led to massive increases in productivity and finances. All the inhabitants saw increases in lifestyle.

What does ancient economic history do with building an Introduction Based business? Everything.

Those ancient farmers knew they needed to plant seeds to harvest crops over time.

Adam Smith knew people needed to exchange goods and services with other specialists freely.

Farmers would trade crops for tools made by tool-making experts, which they would then use to raise more crops, increasing their production more efficiently. This was true in ancient Sumeria, 18th-century Scotland, and today wherever you are. The question is, are you in free exchange with others who can benefit you?

As we explored in the article The Economics of Capitalism for Financial Advisors, the free exchange of goods and/or services for a profit is the core idea of capitalism and the reason why we are in business. Yet, have you established relationships for the exchange of value, trading partners as it were, to increase your production?

Establish Centers of Influence (COIs) for your business.

And don't fall into the twin traps of expecting everything or getting nothing from your Centers.

Centers of Influence are exchanges for ideas and Introductions.

Remember that you earn the right to Introductions by providing value. This value for your Center could be you providing them with Introductions (i.e., if you are a Real Estate Agent, sending business to the roofer, plumber, and painters), or it could be you giving them ideas (like a Financial Advisor bringing the idea of a springing value trust to the attorney or CPA, so they have an additional planning tool to serve their clients and generate additional revenue). Do not expect the COI to hand you value if you are not creating value for them and their clients. Too many people expect to be given things without giving them first. Remember: free EXCHANGE of goods and services. It must go both ways or else it is not a profitable relationship, and the Center will collapse.

The opposing dilemma is giving without ever receiving. If you hand a Center five, eight, or ten Introductions with nothing coming back, there is a problem. It is an issue if you give your Center ideas that they use with their clients and generate tens of thousands of dollars in fees and you get no Introductions or business back. If you bring them their biggest new client and don't get the opportunity to meet new potential clients from them, you are being screwed. Call them out on it.

Tell them straight up, "I have handed you X. Capitalism is the free exchange of goods and services, and there are other professionals who provide your service who would love to work with my clients and will reciprocate with introductions to help me grow my business." Alpha up and have that conversation. If they don't start sending you Introductions/work, then replace them.

Unrequited love in business hurts as much as in other relationships.

As Ben Franklin did with the development of his junta in Pre-Revolutionary Philadelphia, give benefits to others that can professionally benefit you and build your business. Franklin became one of the wealthiest Americans of his time because he developed Centers of Influence that helped drive his printing business. He planted seeds, helped others, and gathered the fruits of those labors over time. The idea of planting, growing, and trading was the key to the earliest civilizations that financed one of our greatest Founding Fathers and should be applied in your business today.

Sit down with a piece of paper. Write down five people who could dramatically impact your production by providing you with a stream of business. Is it the priest who does the pre-Cana for couples about to be married? The Career Counselor? The tech lead in that company, or the HR manager? How about the coach or the VC? Who are the five who could create a constant stream of new Introductions?

Now, how can you help THEM? What value can you bring to them to enhance their business or career? What ideas, what Introductions, what can you do for them to make them better and EARN the seeds to plant for future harvests?

Get out and start becoming a civilized professional.

Start building an Introduction Based Business by planting some seeds.

Multi-Channel Thought Processes and Cognitive Dissonance in Client Communication

The most advanced communication networks on the planet and the human mind are analogous in many ways, and the root of their power also gives rise to some seemingly irrational thoughts and discussions we have with clients. Let's explore the concepts of cognitive dissonance and wavelength division multiplexing as the source of the seemingly irrational conversations and dumb decisions our clients apparently make repeatedly.

Wavelength Division Multiplexing (WDM) is a concept that has enabled the explosion of telecommunications over the past two decades, driving data transfer costs down to the point of allowing essentially unlimited movement of information and the productivity and wealth that it engenders. By being able to send many slightly different signals simultaneously through a communication fiber that does not interact nor interfere with each other, WDM empowers multiple individual discussions to occur simultaneously over the same physical space in a way that would have been incomprehensible two generations ago. A single optical fiber can carry 1.6+ TERRABITS of information a second, the equivalent of about four thousand books or fifteen minutes of Netflix streaming. This is being pumped through a sliver of glass thinner than a human hair every second.

Cognitive Dissonance, on the other hand, is *"a situation involving conflicting attitudes, beliefs or behaviors. This produces a feeling of mental discomfort...*" as stated by Simply Psychology. It arises because the incredibly powerful processor between our ears, capable of one thousand trillion calculations per second (a petaflop), or over 10,000 the computational power of the best computers, doesn't rectify all information. There are disparities we hold in our heads (like believing murder is wrong but supporting the death penalty or that all politicians are corrupt except your buddy, the local politician). Because of the power of our minds, we can construct a reality where two oppositional ideas are non-contrary depending upon how we look at them. In scenarios where two unaligned belief systems come into contact for a situation (say, "I don't give referrals because all people that ask for them are slimy salespeople", but then they meet highly professional You and You are asking for introductions) it is difficult to rectify and somewhat painful when two opposing thought systems interact internally. Essentially, the WDM in our head has broken down, and there is the interaction of the different thoughts/ beliefs that were previously siloed. This interaction often leads to irrationality and apparently dumb decisions from smart people.

When we work with a client, we are having a discussion that is essentially on a single wavelength in their head. But there are simultaneously hundreds if not thousands of other processes going on, from as routine as breathing to as intellectually engaging as trying to figure out where they met you before and what they want for dinner. As Stolk and Templin discuss in "Choices: Creating a Financial Services Career", most people have the capacity for seven plus or minus 2 active cognitive processes operating in parallel. Many of these are engaged with issues we are not seeing, such as trouble with a teenage child, work-related stress, and other unseen issues that literally fill some of their major bandwidth. This creates opportunities to influence and control the remaining major channels in ways we won't discuss here and the opportunity to intentionally cross-communicate channels and force cognitive dissonance to yield an outcome favorable to the advisor.

When a client goes through cognitive dissonance, the thought with the greatest current emotional grounding will dominate in the short term. "I don't give introductions", even if based upon some rationality of experience, can crumble (at least temporarily) in the mental bath of positive emotions from your interaction with them, supplemented by a logical explanation breaking down that argument and the If/Then upfront contract we discussed in a previous post section. Forcing cognitive dissonance is like having a totally overpowered signal going through the fiber optic telecommunication cable that, for a brief moment, overwhelms all other signals that are there, swamping the WDM and getting through the system. This is your intent: to **force a cognitive dissonance** so that they feel the discomfort from the multiple signals and temporarily accept your overdriven message on your professionality and worthiness of introductions.

Even after the fact, the supercomputer in their head will build rationality around why You deserve introductions even though they don't give introductions. Suppose this rational framework is built on sound logic around your professionality and the disproportionate value you have delivered (as we discussed here insert link) reinforced with positive emotions and hope for them achieving the relevant and visceral goal with you. In that case, the memory will be strongly encoded in their brain and belief system. This could create a further incongruity in their thoughts: no one deserves introductions except You. Don't doubt the power of this to protect your client from less professional potential competition.

The opposite can also be true: if they feel you used sales trickery to weasel introductions out of them without giving them an incredible experience and delivering on your initial promises to them, the client will feel taken advantage of and build an internally coherent rationale around you manipulating them for your own benefit. The secret is to make sure you do what you said you would do and be the archetype of professional and helpful. Do your job so well that they cannot doubt you, and in their mind, they will turn you into the hero you are.

Pain is a Barrier

I had the chance to see an interesting speaker, strongman Dave Whitley, aka The Iron Tamer.

This man not only bent a 16-penny nail and ripped a deck of cards in half with his bare hands, but he also discussed the psychology of self-imposed limitations that prevent us from breaking our chains and achieving excellence.

The Marines say, *"Pain is weakness leaving the body."*

Benjamin Franklin stated, *"There are no gains without pains."*

Strongman Slim "The Hammer Man" was insightful when he explained WHY we stop before our full potential, be it bending steel or hitting the Top of The Table through introduction-based production. He said, *"It's not that you don't have the power; it's that you can't get the power out because of fear. The power is there, inside you. The question is, how do you bring it out?"*

How do you go beyond the fear into the glory that awaits on the other side?

One way is to follow Tim Ferriss' favorite approach of fear setting, where instead of focusing on the goal, you explore what is THE absolute worst thing that can happen and how you can recover from it. For those of us in financial services, most of the time, the biggest downside is that they say "no," and our ego gets momentarily bruised. I have yet to have a potential client pull a weapon on me, call a manager, or take out a billboard declaring I am slime. The worst thing that ever happened is someone said "no." But as ultrarunner David Goggins says, it will callous your feelings and eventually won't hurt anymore being rejected.

The outcome of asking for introductions or calling that potential huge client at WORST is that some people say "no," and you become mentally stronger. There is no physical damage, no big financial losses, nothing more than a small slap to the ego that stings for a moment, and then you move on by mentally saying "next."

And if they say "yes"? Potentially life-changing for the better.

That is a very low risk for a high potential return, a great investment if ever there were one.

Sit down and think of all the bad stuff so you can face your fears in the business.

Once you start really looking at them, you realize that they aren't that scary, not like foot-long spiders with glowing red eyes and fangs dripping poison….

Now THAT is something to fear, even more so than fear itself.

A second approach is to take micro-actions for success. Because movement overcomes fear.

How do we eat an elephant?

One bite at a time.

How do we write $500k of premium in a year?

By looking at our business, seeing what is most profitable, and planning to increase the amount of those activities to a level where the output of the daily work sums up to $500k or whatever the goal is that will take you through that barrier of fear to the glory on the other side.

Let's say that your best clients are young attorneys, and currently you average about $2k of business off of them a year each. Can you overcome your fear of hard work and success to work with 250 this year?

Probably not. Just being honest.

But can you:

1. Increase the amount of business you write on each one by doing additional lines of business (investments, disability insurance, property and casualty, etc.)? This increases production by maybe 25% per person.

2. Could you increase your average revenue per client by working with clients in this space who make more money (ones who are more experienced, specialized, older, or in a different physical location)? This could easily increase the average premium per client by 15-20%.

3. Should we build escalators for future production, such as COLA (cost of living adjustments) and guaranteed purchase options? I know dozens of producers who make MDRT just off of this component every single year.

4. Rework your planning cycle to take less time so that you can cycle through more introductions a year, thus producing more business in the same amount of time/meetings.

5. Tweak your process to increase your flow-through rate from Introduction to Client.

6. And, of course, should you use what this book teaches you to get tons more introductions to these people?

Let's say you produced $100k last year, with a 12:1 introduction-to-client ratio and $2k per client business.

Applying the above concepts can increase your production per client to $3k, and practice can bring your sales ratio down to 10:1, as laid out in other posts on this site.

As we have worked through this mental exercise, your fear has dissipated like the morning mist because firing up your neocortex disables most of the fear circuitry in your brain. But even though we have eliminated most of the fear, let's continue the exercise because you might as well keep going and get to that $500k production!

$500k on $3000 per client is 167 clients. Huge job. Absolutely monstrous and in a different plane of existence than what you are doing now. But let's keep going.

With 167 clients, 1,670 introductions are needed on a 10:1 ratio. That's 8 introductions a day for 210 work days in a year. If you keep 2 meetings per day, that is 4 introductions per meeting. Can you do that?

I know you have gotten four introductions in a meeting before. Do it again.

Use an agenda and feeder lists. Pick up the phone more and tweak your confirmation process. Do all of it because you have done 8 in a day before and can do so again and again, especially if you move from 2 kept a day to 2.25 to 2.5 to 3 kept in a day (which is only 4.5 contact hours per day. What are you doing with the rest of your time?).

Will you get to a half million of production in the next twelve months?

Probably not, because I doubt you will quintuple your business due to infrastructure shortfalls and just plain not being used to working that hard. I bet you The Iron Tamer didn't start out bending 16-penny nails, and his tendons and muscles needed to develop over time.

But if you can start getting four introductions at a meeting, just once a day, I guarantee your business will be much stronger in three months. And if you do it once a day, you can get to do it more often, and your number of appointments kept a day will grow quarter by quarter. From the repetition, your skills will strengthen, so your revenue per client will increase.

Soon, you won't remember the fears that kept you below MDRT and from producing and unleashing your power. You'll be knocking on the door of Court of the Table and beyond.

As your internal structure toughens from lifting weights, so too will your mental resolve from facing your fears of failure and failing more often to succeed. Bend the world to your will.

Push through the pain.

Push through to the glory.

Because pain is merely a barrier in your mind, a paper-thin wall in your psyche keeping you from greatness and glory.

SKILL SET

Push on through to the other side.

When you're going through Hell, keep on going. Heaven awaits beyond the veil of tears.

Break your that wall, break those chains.

Break the barrier.

Scout Camp

I spent last week as a volunteer range officer at Cub Scout Camp Wakpominee and relearned some valuable lessons for all professionals, especially those who gain new clients via word of mouth, about creating an Introduction-Based Business.

First and most important is the Scout Motto: Be Prepared. How many times could you have done a better job for your client if you had allocated a little more time researching beforehand? How many introductions have you lost because you didn't take the ten minutes to create an agenda and prep a feeder list? What business have you lost because you were not mentally ready to ask for it? As Lord Baden Powell stated when asked, "prepared for what?": "Why, for any old thing! A true professional has planned for all contingencies."

Secondly, you must aim for something. On the archery range, we don't just fire arrows randomly. We have a target with a bullseye. It's the same with slingshots, BB guns, or .22 caliber rifles. We know what we want (to hit the target, hopefully, the bullseye), and we aim for it. We focus on the goal. If you aren't aiming, you won't hit your target, or worse yet, hit something you don't want to.

Visualize, then shoot!

Thirdly, progress is to be celebrated. We had twin five-year-old girls on the range. Both the bows and the BB guns were as big as they were. But they listened intently and focused, and even though their first attempts missed the targets, they didn't give up. By their second rounds, they were close, and by the end of each session, they were Annie Oakley. They listened to instructions, believed they could do it, and continuously improved. Is a 3-foot-tall five-year-old more committed to improving than you are?

And fourth, stay hydrated. As poet Alexander Pope proclaimed:

" A little learning is a dangerous thing.

Drink deep, or taste not the Pierian spring."

Keep watering your soul, be it by volunteering to help kids with your local foodbank or your professional association. Give of yourself freely in an environment where you can learn from others (even if they are five years old) and you will grow professionally.

Like most things, my week at Scout Camp was harder than I expected and more rewarding. Take the next week, put yourself in that mentality, and see how prepared you are to start hitting the bullseyes in your career.

Hot

It's hot out.

Do something different that draws attention to yourself in a cool way.

Have an ice cream cake delivered to that huge potential client.

Use your social media to post refreshing recipes.

Set up a lemonade stand and staff it with cute kids. I'll even loan you mine.

Try something completely different. Your clients and their associates will say, "Wow, that's cool," and talk about it.

Call your local ice cream truck, and have them swing through your target neighborhood or office park.

Declare "Beachwear Week", dress in Hawaiian shirts, and have inflatable sharks and palm trees outside. Hold all your meetings under the palm tree and change your Zoom background to a beach. Make sure you play lots of Jimmy Buffet.

By mixing it up, your clients will talk about you, and as Barnum said, all publicity is good. It will also excite you and your staff, which will carry over to your productivity. In the middle of winter, you will have numerous pictures and stories to recapture that energy and create new discussions.

SKILL SET

Maybe I'm still suffering from heat exhaustion from this weekend, but I think my clients would look at me as more human than a planning machine if they knew that we were having an inflatable kiddie pool at the office in the depths of the heat wave with virgin strawberry daiquiris for anyone who brought a friend in to meet us.

When it's wicked hot, be the cool kid.

Thoughts on Thoughts

Great things are made up of little things, whether a cathedral is built of individual stones, a Lego Death Star is built from individual blocks, or the world around us is constructed of atoms. All things are built off of a vast collection of tiny pieces, and our lives are exactly this way, too. But our lives are built in our minds instead of being built by blocks made in a factory.

Years ago, I worked with a sports psychologist named Pete Greider, who had worked with the St. Louis Cardinals and various NBA teams. One of the demos he did during a talk was to show the sheer volume of our thoughts. He dropped a metal BB onto a steel plate, and it rolled into a container, representing a single thought.

He then opened the upper chamber to release all 50,000 BBs, streaming down for several minutes in a hammering cacophony reflective of what we do stretch out over a day. Thousands of thoughts an hour, every day. 95% of these thoughts for most people are repetitive. 80% are negative.

We tell ourselves over and over and over, 40,000 times a day negative things.

No wonder we are beaten down and make poor decisions; we have a critic in our heads constantly berating us and tearing us down. This is not a good thing.

Change your thoughts and change your life.

Expose yourself to some positive reinforcement in the morning (like reading, meditative music, or positive statements; I use YouTube while working out), and you can drop that negative proportion pretty dramatically, leading to a better attitude and outcome.

Canadian psychotherapist Jordan Peterson mentions in "12 Rules for Living" that we make 500-1000 decisions a day based on those 50,000 thoughts. If 80% of the thoughts are negative, it is reasonable to assume that 80+ % of our decisions will be suboptimal because of the negative biases and stresses we have internally. There are 400-800+ poor micro-decisions (and a few major ones) daily.

As a pledge in my Fraternity decades ago, I was taught to make the least bad choice.

Generally, we have two options on most choices (*"Do or Do Not,"* to quote Yoda). The easy choice or the fulfilling one. Current, momentary pleasure or deferred gratification. The harder choice is almost always, the better one overall, but we are constantly seduced by the "just" (I'm just having one cookie, I'm just hitting the snooze button, I'm just missing doing x for today, I'm just looking for some excitement, etc.) instead of the right one.

If we could make a handful of better decisions daily, even on the micro level, it would shift our Good/Poor choice ratio by a full percent. That is not a huge deal and only takes a few seconds and some tiny action alterations. But if you were a single percent better today than you were yesterday, it would slow your descent into the pits.

And in a few days make a few more good decisions on average and get a percent better again.

Further, slow the decline. Maybe even pause it.

And then again, a few better micro-decisions about what we put in our bodies or minds, how we choose to spend time, and with whom. Another 1% swing, maybe in the positive direction.

A few more tiny, better choices lead to the once-in-a-while big decision for the excellent outcome rather than the convenient one. One big, good decision can be a difference-maker overall.

You are creating better micro habits that can compound and reinforce and lead to further better decisions, a positive flywheel in motion as discussed in *Good to Great* by Jim Collins.

You change the destination of a rocket by tiny adjustments to the path that, over thousands or tens of thousands of miles, produces a radically different destination. Same too with ourselves. Little course corrections yield ending up in a good place instead of a bad one. Those course corrections are swapping some of the negative thoughts for positive ones and the bad choices for better ones. Nothing radical, but the consistently slow improvement over the days, months, and years.

Imagine the You of a few years hence with these small micro-decisional improvements. What does your body feel like and look like? What is your educational and professional achievement? How do your relationships look? When in a while the majority of your little and big decisions improve your life instead of harming it, how much wealthier do you believe you will feel across whatever dimension you wish to look at?

It will be good, maybe even great. Because you got your positive choice flywheel going through little incremental decisions and pushes. The little things matter.

Better BBs. Better building blocks. Better thoughts to build more optimal decisions. Little constant choices to be better or ultimately bitter.

You get to build your future with your thoughts and choices. Think about that.

Scout Sale Story

This is to all my new friends (including those I have not yet met) in the financial services world, especially those who complain about being broke or not having enough people to see.

I spent Saturday and Sunday in the cold outside a store with the Cub Scouts, selling popcorn. It was my son's sixth birthday, and he still worked because he really wanted to earn that fishing lure and knew he had a responsibility to the Pack.

He and his brother know what they want, and they know they are going to have to work to get it. We don't believe in trophies for participation in anything less than a half marathon. I will reward consistent hard effort because of the habit it builds, but not just showing up and expecting others to do your job.

This scrawny, hyperactive six-year-old with zero attention span spent his birthday asking everyone who walked into the store, "Would you like to buy popcorn or make a donation to support Cub Scouts Pack 2?" Every single person.

His brother then asked everyone to walk out of the store. Every. Last. One.

In a single day, my boys hit their basic fundraising goal. And they were back the next day, because they hadn't reached THEIR goal. Nor are they done.

If you are complaining about being in the financial services industry, ask yourself these questions:

1. Do I have my scripts memorized? Like by heart.
2. How much have I practiced? That six-year-old now has more sales experience than most 2nd year agents in terms of number of asks.
3. Am I consistently asking? Like no one got past these kids without being asked to buy popcorn or make a donation to Pack 2.
4. Do I have a WHY? Why am I doing this? A fishing lure and trip can motivate a kid, what motivates you?
5. Are you actually working?

I saw a Brian Tracy video that said the average salesperson works only about 90 minutes a day. From my observations, he is slightly low, but no more than a bad sitcom's worth of time a day. My kids definitely were active nonstop in sales mode for over six hours solid. You can do half that; you are three times his size!

So, if your appointment book isn't full, why not stand in front of a store for an hour, hand out your card, and say, "Life insurance is now on sale. You might want to talk to me later this week." In one hour, you will have more results than an hour of cold calling and more fortitude for doing so.

You might also get a bright and shiny fishing lure.

Morning Joe

The other day I needed coffee. Badly.

I had a couple of major presentations and had worked late and was up early.

I tried to make coffee in the pot at the office. I used fresh ground (thank you, Kevin, at Upstate Coffee!), added water, and started. Then I went to my office to take care of a few moments of stuff.

The weird gurgling sounds like if The Tank Gang were trying a breakout in Finding Nemo. I came out of my office to find spewed coffee and grounds all over the place. Luckily, there was no fish gasping for breath, but a mess that a toddler would be proud of—and no consumable coffee.

So, I threw on my coat, drove over to a Starbucks, pulled aside because a client called, and twenty minutes later, I pulled around to the order kiosk. My Blood Caffeine Content was dangerously low.

Temporarily closed.

Dang.

Or more like "@%#^@$@%&$%&", sounding like Qbert from the video game.

I drive in the other direction and get coffee. Actually, I got three, just to be safe.

Good thing, due to a scheduling error my presentation was an hour later than initially planned, and man did I need that caffeine.

So here is what I wish for you: I wish you were as committed to getting Introductions as I was to get my coffee. I was told "no" twice, but did I give up?

Nope!

Reformulated my approach and went back at it.

Didn't give up in the face of adversity.

Got what I needed to run my business.

Do you go three times?

On the phone?

When asking for Introductions or the business?

Why not?

I could have found a substitute for coffee, be it tea, doing a bunch of jumping jacks to get my blood flowing, or eating a scoop of Sriracha sauce. What can you substitute for Intros? Buying the same leads a half-dozen other people are buying? Cold calling all day? Those are lousy substitutes.

Just get the Intros. It's easier and more effective.

And you won't have to clean up the mess like I had to. Just sayin'.

Small Things

Blink-182 sang it best:

"Late night, come home Work sucks, I know She left me roses by the stairs Surprises let me know she cares"

It is all the small things that make the difference in a relationship be it platonic, erotic, or professional.

Does your client take cinnamon cream in her coffee? Make it happen for her.

Is someone having a rough quarter in their biz? Just call and leave a quick message.

Text your client a pic of her favorite flowers after you talk one day.

Greet your client in their other language if they are multilingual.

Your assistant has a kid that gets out of school at 3:30. Early dismissal on Friday if all the work is done so they get that extra special time with their little one.

That potential client has a little trouble hearing. Use a voice-to-text service to help them not miss a beat in a conversation with you.

Send that prospect the info on a weird sports thing you randomly discussed.

Ask your client about their trip.

Send them the pumpkin-spiced latte they mentioned the day before.

Make working with you an experience that your clients want to share, and they will share with you.

As I joke with all of my clients: I might not help you, but the entertainment value is worth the price of admission. And they laugh, knowing what a goofball I am at times but also that they truly are getting great guidance and assistance in addition to its being a humorous experience.

One of the biggest producers I know told me when I was brand new in the business "I do a million little things differently". So do I now, all the small things. So should you, in your own way. Show you are paying attention and that you care.

Do the little things because attention to detail indicates you will do the right thing with the Big Things. Show you care.

Lab Rat

I am a laboratory. A constant experiment in improvement, a forced evolution to make myself better week by week.

I am not the extreme of Tim Ferriss (author of "The 4 Hour Work Week" and "The 4 Hour Body") in that I am not willing to go whole hog on pharmaceuticals and wiring myself up like I'm in the Matrix, but I am willing to run trial runs and tweaks on everything from my language with clients to my physical training to (gulp) even my See Food Diet (See Food, Eat Food!).

Improvement only happens by chance over hundreds of generations from genetic superiority for the environment if we let Mother Nature run her course. I don't have that much time and neither do you. I'm going to give her a push, and not like the High Evolutionary from Marvel Comics. I am going to alter myself in a calculated and focused manner, stress the system (me) to see what results arise, and then evaluate and apply the lessons learned for the next cycle of growth.

Are you willing to force yourself to grow, or are you saying, "Life is good. I'm comfortable. I could get better but it's not worth the effort."? Age and the evolution of the market should neutralize those pitiful arguments as the average person loses about 1% capacity (mental or muscle mass) per year after certain ages, and the world is going to keep moving forward even if you aren't. Small consistent changes are needed to not fall behind, let alone grow and achieve.

SKILL SET

Here are some little things I've figured out so over the past few years to save time, get in the zone quicker, or improve my mental acuity or physical condition.

1. When the alarm goes off in the morning, get out of bed and turn it off. OUT OF THE BED.
2. After the alarm is off, sit on the bed, close your eyes, and think about your goal for the year, then the month, then the week, and then that particular day. Take one minute and visualize hitting the goal of the day. You are still only semiconscious, so this is when your mind is most susceptible to self-talk, and convincing yourself you are hitting today's goal is a great start to the day.
3. Prep the coffee the night before. Run the pot so you have basically a cup (it will be strong) and turn it off. This way you have a cup ready to go, can turn the pot on and have the rest of the pot fresh and ready when you are done with the first cup, and be productive several minutes quicker each morning.
4. Morning exercise compound results. Even if it is only 5 minutes while that pot of coffee finishes brewing after your first few sips, it can make your body rev an extra 1% for the day easily.
5. Studies show that a little resistance training (squats, push-ups, planks, actual lifting) before eating reduces insulin spikes, helping to mellow out the peaks and valleys and increase fat burn. So, a few minutes of air squats or isometrics before breakfast, lunch, and dinner are worth 2-3x the time invested.
6. Use YouTube to feed your brain in downtime, like driving.

7. Do all your phone conferences while standing and walking back and forth. Steve Jobs and Frederich Nietzsche approve!

None of these are earth-shattering insights. But they all help and will help your mind, body, and business for almost zero-time cost. But be careful; once you start looking for little ways to improve, you might start thinking about big changes like committing to coaching, eliminating junk food from your house, or actually reading books. It's a slippery slope to self-improvement and metacognition, so be careful!

Passive Introductions

One of the more interesting things we have found over the decades is that all Reps love Passive Introductions, where the client tells you, "By the way, you should call my friend So and So. They just inherited some money and want to talk to someone, so I gave them your name."

Everyone loves getting paid without doing work, so this is not all that interesting.

The interesting thing is that due to the way the brain is wired, everyone disproportionately remembers getting these Passive Introductions, disproportionately valuing them, and expecting them as a way to build their career.

But here's a dirty secret: getting handed Passive Introductions is actually the result of years of hard work. It is like winning the Gold Medal after decades of practice, or the overnight success in Hollywood after five years of waiting tables and couch surfing. Getting passive introductions is like the music superstar that gets invited to appear on various projects, not because they are great now but because of decades of excellence that might not be obvious. The minor league baseball player who toiled and didn't get their shot at the big leagues until they were traded, someone got injured, and all of a sudden, they perform on the big stage, and people say, "Where did they come from?!"

I used to get at least one call each month "Hi, I'm a friend of X Client, and they told me I have to talk to you about my financial planning because you helped them out so much. When can we talk?" Yes, it was great, but 99+% of my Introductions I actually worked for, so if I was counting on that call-in appointment, I'd be doing something else for a living because you simply cannot survive on passive Introductions in the first two or three decades of your career.

Passive Introductions are literally the last 1% of your business, the icing on the cake.

But it is the cream cheese frosting that truly makes carrot cake wonderful and separates it from being a muffin.

So here are some ways to increase your chances of getting Passive Introductions.

1. Change your voicemail. Make sure your voicemail includes the phrase "and don't forget that I work on an Introduction basis." You need to hammer this into your clients' heads so that they think of you and Introductions and excellence in the same synaptic fire.
2. Have your staff always say, "And don't forget, XXX works strictly on an introduction basis." Every time they leave a message for a client your staff should be reinforcing your message.
3. Have it on your website.
4. Talk about it. From the first time you sit down with a potential client to talk about planning, in every meeting with them, and in your correspondence, you should be reminding clients that you work on Introductions instead of cold calling or buying lists or running blast email spam campaigns, because it is more efficient and leaves you more time to service clients or do research to serve them better.

SKILL SET

5. Nest. Focus on getting a bunch of clients who love you in a particular office or company. Be an expert in their benefits and needs, be seen in the office (especially with their leaders), and be known as "Our Finance Guy/Lady." You'll get the call, "Hey, I'm new at SuperDuper Tech, and everyone says I need to talk to you. When are you going to be in our office again?"

These actions are actual work to get Passive Introductions in the future, but it is critical. If you don't sow you can't reap a harvest. If you don't have your clients ACTIVELY involved, you can never be passively involved in getting Introductions.

We used to have clients show up to annual reviews with four typed names with contact info, and they would apologize and say, "We'll get you a fifth today while we are talking." Because they were well trained, we had invested the time to create a CULTURE of Introductions not just among the Reps I mentored and my staff but also among the people I worked with. We worked hard so that we could work easier later.

As Financial Advisors, we talk for a living. Make sure you are talking about Introductions regularly because your clients will eventually pick up on it and want to share it with you. Be consistent with discussing it, be consistent with asking for them, and make it easy for your clients to give you Introductions. Do the hard work now, and it will be easy later. Till the soil today so that you can harvest tomorrow.

4th Quarter Hurry Up

The leaves are changing and falling. The air is crisp, and we have both baseball playoffs and football. Days are growing short, just like the calendar year.

We have entered the fourth quarter of the year, and just like the fourth quarter of a football game, you are probably behind. It's time to implement the hurry-up offense. How can you get a couple of quick scores?

1. Anyone that you asked to take action but who didn't buy in the first half of the year, but didn't say "no, never" should be called.
2. Anyone who bought last calendar year but has not bought this year should be reviewed and talked to.
3. Any of those Introductions that scheduled a meeting, but had to reschedule? Get them back on the books.
4. Call your 10 best clients and ask them each for 1 extremely high-quality individual going through changes in their life.

Short and sweet, quick actions. Now hurry up and go score!

APPENDIX

Unlike your appendix, this one is useful. It contains a variety of things I actually use with clients and have for decades. Modify them as appropriate, and make sure that your Compliance Officer signs off on your using them with clients because I don't want to get sued by you because you didn't get proper approval. My CO signed off on all of these so you shouldn't have much of an issue with taking the core of these and tweaking them a bit to get the imprimatur from your Powers That Be.

Financial Planning Document Checklist Retirement accounts

- 401(k), 403(b), 401(a), 457 and/or other qualified retirement plans
- Traditional IRAs
- Roth IRAs
- SEP IRAs
- SIMPLE IRAs

Cash accounts

- Certificates of deposit (CDs)
- Checking, savings, and money market accounts
- Money market mutual funds

Nonqualified accounts

- Brokerage accounts
- Stock options
- Mutual funds
- Annuities
- Deferred compensation plans

Education funding accounts

- 529 plans
- Coverdell ESAs
- UGMA/UTMAs

Real estate

- Mortgage statement or loan information
- Real estate appraisals
- Property tax statement

Business ownership

- Business tax returns, including schedules
- Business valuation/appraisals
- Buy/sell agreements
- Employee benefits
- Employer-provided retirement plans
- Nonqualified deferred compensation plans

Personal Budget

- Mortgage/home equity loans
- Student loans
- Auto loans
- Credit card debt Income
- Pay statements for the last two pay periods
- Federal and state tax returns for the past two years, including schedules
- W-2 and 1099 documents
- Most recent Social Security statement(s)
- Other income sources
- Expenses/cash flow (if not readily available, please provide a monthly estimate)

Insurance

- Life insurance contracts and most recent statement
- Disability income insurance contracts
- Long-term care insurance contract
- Medical, homeowner's, auto insurance, and liability (umbrella) contracts
- Employee benefits information/booklet

Estate and legal documents

- Copy of will, trust, or other documents
- Copy of power of attorney and health care directive

Name and Date

5. Introductions
6. Overview of Process
7. Mutual Expectations
8. Information Gathering
    a. Facts
    b. Feelings
    c. Philosophies
9. Clarification of Goals & Objectives
10. Red Flags
11. Favorable Introductions
12. Next Appointment:

Expected Time of Meeting: 90 minutes.

AGENDA: PRESENTATION MEETING

Name and Date

1. Review of Goals and Objectives
2. Review of Analysis
3. Recommendations
4. Implementation Decision:
   - a. Yes
   - b. No
   - c. Need Additional Information:
5. Execution Steps
6. Favorable Introductions
7. Next Appointment:

Expected Time of Meeting: 90 minutes.

Introduction Brainstorming Questions

For Business Owner, September 23, 2024

Who are your best Suppliers?

Who are your best Customers?

Who are your most ambitious friends?

Who are the three people who have inspired you the most in your business career?

If you were assembling your Board of Directors, who would you pick to be on the Board and why?

One of the keys to building a successful business is surrounding yourself with excellence.

Please let us know who else you need from our network to help you grow.

Introduction Classifications

DATE

CLIENT NAME

Richard X Pat

Dan Moseley

Heather Patenaude

Matthieu Blows

Jay Lipps

Y. R. American

Olivia Ribley

Royal Cuiloi

Lora Liar

Note:

Names in Italics indicate existing relationships.

Names in Bold indicate strongly desired Introductions.

Recommended Books

Clear, James. 2018. *Atomic Habits: An Easy & Proven Way to Build Good Habits & Break Bad Ones.* https://catalog.umj.ac.id/index.php?p=show_detail&id=62390.

Collins, Jim. 2009. "*Good to Great - (Why Some Companies Make the Leap and Others Don't)*." NHRD Network Journal 2 (7): 102–5. https://doi.org/10.1177/0974173920090719.

Csikszentmihalyi, Mihaly. 2009. *Flow: The Psychology of Optimal Experience.* Harper Collins.

Ferriss, Timothy. 2011. *The 4-Hour Work Week: Escape the 9-5, Live Anywhere and Join the New Rich.* Random House.

Laozi. 1996. *Tao Te Ching.* Wordsworth Editions.

Mandino, Og. 2011. *The Greatest Salesman in the World.* Bantam.

Peterson, Jordan B. 2018. *12 Rules for Life: An Antidote to Chaos.* Penguin UK.

Thomson, Andrew H. 2019. *The Feldman Method.* Blurb.

Tolkien, J. R. R. 2024. *The Lord of the Rings Collector's Edition Box Set: Includes the Fellowship of the Ring, the Two Towers, and the Return of the King.* William Morrow.

Tzu, Sun. 2002. *The Art of War.* Courier Corporation.

Willink, Jocko. 2020. *Discipline equals freedom: Field Manual* Mk1-MOD1. St. Martin's Press.

Willink, Jocko, and Leif Babin. 2024. *The dichotomy of leadership: Balancing the Challenges of Extreme Ownership to Lead and Win* (Expanded Edition). St. Martin's Press.

Recommended Articles

Francisco Saez- "Good Street, Bad Stress"

Christopher Bergland- "Cortisol: Why the "Stress Hormone" Is Public Enemy No. 1"

Asha Pandey- "6 Killer Examples of Gamification in eLearning"

John Hahn- "After Debilitating Spinal Injury, NFL's Ryan Shazier Walks Onstage During Draft Night: 'Incredible'"

Kendra Cherry- "What Are the Big 5 Personality Traits?"

Heather Long- "American professor wins Nobel Prize in economics for trying to understand bad human behavior."

Deborah Smith- "Psychologist wins Nobel Prize Daniel Kahneman is honored for bridging economics and psychology."

For additional insight, feel free to research more about these concepts.

Gamification

Boolean Logic

Sandler Sales System

Cognitive Dissonance

Wavelength Division Multiplexing

Printed in the USA
CPSIA information can be obtained
at www.ICGtesting.com
LVHW020930030924
789973LV00013B/523